James Ross Snowden

The Cornplanter Memorial

An historical sketch of Gy-ant-wa-chia - the Cornplanter, and of the six nations of Indians

James Ross Snowden

The Cornplanter Memorial
An historical sketch of Gy-ant-wa-chia - the Cornplanter, and of the six nations of Indians

ISBN/EAN: 9783337307868

Printed in Europe, USA, Canada, Australia, Japan

Cover: Foto ©ninafisch / pixelio.de

More available books at **www.hansebooks.com**

THE CORNPLANTER MEMORIAL.

AN HISTORICAL SKETCH

OF

Gy-ant-wa-chia — The Cornplanter,

AND OF THE

SIX NATIONS OF INDIANS.

BY JAMES ROSS SNOWDEN.

AND THE REPORT OF

SAMUEL P. JOHNSON,

ON THE ERECTION OF THE MONUMENT AT JENNESADAGA, TO THE MEMORY OF CORNPLANTER.

Published by order of the Legislature of Pennsylvania.

HARRISBURG, PA:
SINGERLY & MYERS, STATE PRINTERS.
1867.

NOTE.

SENATE OF PENNSYLVANIA,
Harrisburg, March 15, 1867.

THE report of Hon. SAMUEL P. JOHNSON, on the completion of the monument authorized by the last Legislature, to be erected to the memory of CORNPLANTER, a Chief of the Six Nations, having been presented to the Senate, by Senator BROWN, of Mercer, the following resolution was adopted:

Resolved, That one thousand copies of said report, together with the historical sketch, with accompanying documents, prepared by Hon. JAMES ROSS SNOWDEN, be printed, and that the thanks of the Legislature be presented to these gentlemen for the able and satisfactory manner in which they have discharged the duties assigned them.

PREFATORY.

A joint resolution of the Legislature of Pennsylvania was passed on the 7th day of March, 1867, inviting Hon. JAMES ROSS SNOWDEN to deliver, in the Hall of the House of Representatives, his historical address on CORNPLANTER and the Six Nations of Indians.

Pursuant to this resolution, on the 14th of March, the members of both Houses, and a number of citizens, being convened, Hon. JOHN P. GLASS, Speaker of the House of Representatives, was called to the chair; and GEO. W. HAMERSLY, Esq., Clerk of the Senate, A. W. BENEDICT, Esq., Clerk of the House of Representatives, and JOHN A. SMULL, Esq., Resident Clerk of the House of Representatives, were appointed Secretaries.

Mr. SNOWDEN was introduced to the audience by Mr. Speaker GLASS, with some appropriate remarks.

Previous to the delivery of the historical sketch, Mr. SNOWDEN made the following introductory remarks:

At the last session of the Legislature a joint resolution was adopted, appropriating a sum of money for the erection of a monument to the memory of CORNPLANTER, the celebrated Chief of the Seneca Nation of Indians. The same resolution placed the subject in charge of the Hon. SAMUEL P. JOHNSON, President Judge of the Sixth Judicial District. Under his direction, an appropriate monument was prepared and placed in position over the grave of the Chief, at Jennesadaga, (Cornplanter's village,) in the county of Warren, on the Allegheny river, fifteen miles above the borough of Warren. I was selected, by Judge JOHNSON, to deliver an address upon the occasion. This duty I performed. The monument was dedicated

PREFATORY.

with appropriate exercises, on the 18th of October last. There were present about four hundred Indians, and a large concourse of citizens of Pennsylvania and New York.

I have, at hand, the report of Judge JOHNSON, to the Legislature, showing the manner in which he has discharged the duties assigned him. His report embraces his introductory remarks and the historical sketch which I delivered. Also, the responses made by a Chief of the Six Nations, and a councillor of the Seneca Nation. The responses were made in the Indian language. They were reported, and taken down by me as they were translated by an interpreter at the time of delivery.

I have here, also, a photograph of the monument and the audience, taken during the delivery of the historical address. This report, with the accompanying papers, will be presented to the Legislature. I am here, this evening, at the request of the Senate and House of Representatives, to deliver the historical and biographical sketch which I pronounced at the grave of CORNPLANTER, when the monument, erected to his memory, was dedicated. For the honor of this invitation, I beg to present to the members of the Legislature my sincere thanks.

After Mr. SNOWDEN had concluded his address, the following resolutions, offered by Senator M. B. LOWRY, of Erie, and seconded by Senator THOMAS J. BIGHAM, of Allegheny, were unanimously adopted:

Resolved, That the members of the House of Representatives, jointly assembled, hereby tender our thanks to the Hon. JAMES ROSS SNOWDEN, for his excellent and carefully prepared historical address, prepared for and delivered on the occasion of the dedication of the CORNPLANTER monument, and which we have heard repeated with lively interest and satisfaction.

Resolved further, That the thanks of the members of both Houses is also tendered to Hon. SAMUEL P. JOHNSON, for the judicious and admirable manner in which he has discharged the duty assigned him, by the last Legislature, in causing to be erected an appropriate and suitable monument over the grave of the Seneca Chief.

Resolved, That copies of these resolutions be furnished to Colonel SNOWDEN and Judge JOHNSON; and that the same be prefixed to the publication of the CORNPLANTER memorial.

JOHN P. GLASS, *President.*

ATTEST:

A. W. BENEDICT,
GEO. W. HAMERSLY, } *Secretaries.*
JOHN A. SMULL,

CONTENTS.

1. Report of S. P. JOHNSON.
2. Historical sketch, by J. R. SNOWDEN.
3. Speech of JOHN LUKE, Councillor of the Seneca Nation.
4. Speech of STEPHEN S. SMITH, Chief of the Six Nations.
5. Appendices, containing speeches of CORNPLANTER, and address of WASHINGTON to CORNPLANTER.
6. Statement of the present condition of the Six Nations.

REPORT OF HON. S. P. JOHNSON.

To the Senate and House of Representatives
of the Commonwealth of Pennsylvania:

AT the last session of the Legislature a joint resolution was passed by your honorable bodies, appropriating five hundred dollars, for the erection of a monument to the memory of CORNPLANTER, an Indian Chief of the Seneca tribe, whose remains were deposited at Jennesadaga, where he had resided, in the county of Warren. By said resolution, I was appointed to superintend the execution of this generous purpose.

This duty might have been committed to more competent, but not more willing hands. My personal relations with the venerated chieftain in his life-time, had left a vivid recollection of his virtues that the abrasion of more than thirty years could not obliterate.

In discharge of the duty thus imposed, I procured a monument of marble, to be erected by Mr. W. H. FULLERTON, of South Dorset, Vermont. In size, design and workmanship, it more than met my expectation, and was very creditable to the artificer. The monument itself, of beautiful Vermont marble, is over eleven feet high, and stands on a handsomely cut native stone base, four feet in diameter, by one and a-half feet deep. It is located immediately between the grave of CORNPLANTER, and that of his wife, from whom he was separated by death but about three months. On the second section are four well carved dies, in the form of a shield. Upon the spire facing west, is cut in large raised letters

"GIANTWAHIA, THE CORNPLANTER."

Upon the die on the same side, is inscribed,

"JOHN O'BAIL *alias* CORNPLANTER, *died at Cornplanter town, February 18, 1836, aged about 100 years.*"

On the die fronting south, the following inscription is handsomely lettered:

"*Chief of the Seneca tribe, and a principal Chief of the Six Nations, from the period of the Revolutionary war, to the time of his death. Distinguished for talents, courage, eloquence, sobriety and love of his tribe and race, to whose welfare he devoted his time, his energies and his means, during a long and eventful life.*"

On the die upon the East side is engraved—

"ERECTED BY AUTHORITY OF THE LEGISLATURE OF PENNSYLVANIA, BY ACT JANUARY 25, 1866."

Desiring to make the munificence of the State as gratifying to the family and friends of the good old Chief as possible, I appointed a time for the erection and dedication of the monument, and was fortunate enough to procure the services of Col. JAMES ROSS SNOWDEN, of Philadelphia, to prepare an address suitable to the occasion, commemorative of the character and services of the distinguished Chief.

These ceremonies took place on the 18th of October last, in presence of the family and decendants of CORNPLANTER, about eighty in number, and a large assembly of native Indians, remnants of the once formidable Six Nations, from the Allegheny, Cattaraugus and Tonnawanda reservations in the State of New York, and also a large concourse of the pale faces from the surrounding country. Everything went off most satisfactorily, and to the high gratification of our aboriginal friends. The exercises of the day were conducted according to the following programme:

1. Invocatory prayer by the Chaplain.
2. Introductory address by your representative, as master of ceremonies.
3. Dedicatory address, by Hon. JAMES ROSS SNOWDEN.
4. Address on the personal character of CORNPLANTER, and the lessons it taught, by Rev. W. A. RANKIN.
5. Responsive addresses, in the Seneca language, by JOHN LUKE, of the Cattaraugus reservation, a Councillor of the Seneca Nations, and by the Rev. STEPHEN S. SMITH, a native of the Tonnawanda reservation, Gennessee county, N. Y., also a Seneca chief of the Six Nations.

These two latter addresses, as also those made by the Rev. Mr. RANKIN and myself, were interpreted, as delivered, by HARRISON HALFTOWN and another educated native of the Seneca nation. Before the dedicatory services commenced, the assembly was addressed in the Seneca language, by SOLOMON O'BAIL, a grandson of CORNPLANTER, and a chief of his tribe, dressed in the full regalia of aboriginal royalty.

Three of CORNPLANTER'S children still survive, and were present to enjoy the occasion; and, by them, I was solemnly charged to communicate to your honorable bodies, their sincere and reiterated thanks for the distinguished honor thus rendered to their beloved ancestor. I have seldom seen deeper gratitude in human hearts than swelled the bosoms of these now venerable children, and those of many grand-children of the hero, whose virtues and memory it has delighted you to honor.

Of the excellent music, by a native brass band, that enlivened the occasion, the pic-nic that followed, and the exciting war dance, that closed the exercises of the day, I will not stop to speak.

There remains yet in my hands, unexpended, about $45 of the appropriation made. The lateness of the season, the paucity of funds and the pressure of other engagements, combined to prevent the erection of such an enclosure around the monument as the Legislature evidently contemplated, and as would be suitable for its permanent protection.

To construct such a fence, of imperishable material, as ought to surround this memorial of State gratitude, to a public benefactor, will require at least $100, judiciously expended. I think it is due to the credit of the State, as it would be highly pleasing to the heirs and friends of CORNPLANTER, that a small additional appropriation should be made to consistently complete the work so generously begun. I am willing to bestow my time and attention, gratuitously, to accomplish it. I append to this report, the introductory remarks made at the dedication ceremonies, and the excellent address delivered by Col. SNOWDEN, together with brief sketches of the responses made by the native orators who graced the occasion, that you may make such a disposition of them as, in your judgment, may be creditable to the State and beneficial to posterity.

S. P. JOHNSON.

WARREN, *January* 25, 1867.

INTRODUCTORY REMARKS

OF

HON. S. P. JOHNSON.

Friends of Cornplanter and fellow citizens:

By a joint resolution of the Pennsylvania Legislature, approved by the Governor the 25th of January, 1866, the State Treasurer was directed to pay to me, the sum of five hundred dollars, " to be expended in erecting and enclosing a suitable monument to CORNPLANTER, as a recognition of his eminent services to the State during its early history."

This duty I have endeavored to perform, as well as the limited means at my disposal would permit. You have before you to-day, the result of that effort, which, for the price paid, is highly creditable to the State, the Chieftain, whose virtues it is intended to commemorate, and the architect who designed and executed it. It is befitting that the virtues and services of public benefactors should receive public recognition and be perpetuated by suitable memorials. There is much in the history of CORNPLANTER, after his alliance with the American government, to elicit admiration and secure the gratitude of this State and the nation.

Immediately upon the close of the Revolutionary war he became the fast friend of the white man and the government. Satisfied that his nation had been fraudulently decoyed into alliance with the British during the war, and basely betrayed by their allies at its close, he hastened to repair the wrong, by giving all his influence and energies to the inauguration of a peace between the United States and the Six Nations, of which he was then a distinguished Chief. Although resisted by all the craftiness of BRANT, and the eloquence of RED JACKET, he persisted until his purpose was consummated by the treaties of Fort Stanwix and Fort Harmar, both of which were secured through and executed by himself. By them the Indian claims to most of the land in Western New York, and North-Western Pennsylvania, was surrendered, and a perpetual peace ordained.

But the great merit of his life, and which most entitled him to the gratitude of the American government, and the State of Pennsylvania, was his successful efforts to prevent the Six Nations uniting in the Confederacy of western Indians formed in 1790–91. Had these tribes, then the most powerful on the continent, joined that Confederacy, the bloody realities of the war that followed, would have spread over the entire western frontier of Pennsylvania, and its termination in 1794, by the victory of General WAYNE, rendered exceedingly doubtful.

General ST. CLAIR anticipated and forwarned against this union, after his defeat in '91, and General KNOX, then Secretary of War, dreaded and fortified against it. But CORNPLANTER, with untiring exertions, and at the hazard of his own life, prevented such a disastrous result, and thus saved the settlers on the Allegheny and upper Ohio, from the horrors of a merciless Indian warfare. For his invaluable services in the procurement and maintenance of peace between his people and the infant nation, just recuperating from its exhausting conflict with the British lion, CORNPLANTER received the thanks and liberal donations of the government and General WASHINGTON.

We are now assembled upon the homestead which CORNPLANTER lived, and where, after an eventful life, during the most eventful period of this continent, he lived and died, at peace with himself, with all the world, and, we trust, with his Merciful Creator. For many years, the appearance of his venerable form, at any point in the Valley of this beautiful river, from its source to its outlet, was the signal for a courteous and kindly greeting by all who knew him. His visitors, whether on business or for curiosity, were always treated with a dignified kindness and hospitality that would have graced the castle of a Duke, in the days of chivalry.

On this beautiful spot, of his own selection, the gift of a grateful Commonwealth for appreciated merit, he spent the last forty-five years of his life, surrounded by his family and descendants, in the practice of all those virtues that adorn both civilized and savage life.

He was the dauntless warrior and wisest statesman of his nation, the patriarch of his tribe and the peacemaker of his race. He was a model man from nature's mould. Truth, temperance, justice and humanity, never had a nobler incarnation or more earnest and consistent advocate than he. As we loved him personally, and revere the noble, manly character he bore, we erect this tribute to his memory, that those who live after us may know and imitate his virtues.

Gy-ant-wa-chia, or Cornplanter,

The last War Chief of the Senecas, and of the Iroquois, or Six Nations.

AN HISTORICAL SKETCH BY

JAMES ROSS SNOWDEN.

GY-ANT-WA-CHIA, OR CORNPLANTER,

The last War Chief of the Senecas, and of the Iroquois, or Six Nations.

AN HISTORICAL SKETCH BY

JAMES ROSS SNOWDEN.

A solitary traveler, after the close of the Revolutionary war, in 1783, wandering near the shores of Chatauque lake,* found himself benighted; and ignorant of the path which should lead him to his place of destination, he feared he would be compelled to pass the night in the forest and without shelter. But when the darkness of the night gathered around him, he saw the light of a distant fire in the woods, to which he immediately bent his steps. There he found an Indian wigwam, the habitation of a Chief with his family. He was kindly received and hospitably entertained. After a supper of corn and venison, the traveler returned thanks to God, whose kind Providence had directed his way, and preserved him in the wilderness. He slept comfortably on the ample bear skins provided by his host.

In the morning the Indian invited the traveler to sit beside him on a large log in front of his cabin. They were seated side by side; presently the Indian told the traveler to move a little; which he did; and, keeping

---

*Cha-da-gweh, by the Senecas; meaning a place where one was lost.

by his side, again requested him to move. This was repeated several times. At length, when near the end of the log, the Chief gave an energetic push, and requested his companion to move further. The traveler remonstrated, and said, "I can go no further; if I do I shall fall off the log." "That is the way," said the Indian, in reply, "that you white people treat us. When the United People, the Six Nations, owned the whole land, from the lakes to the great water, they gave to CORLAER* a seat on the Hudson, and to ONAS† a town and land on the Delaware. We have been driven from our lands on the Mohawk, the Gennessee, the Chemung and the Unadilla. And from our western door we have been pushed, from the Susquehanna, then over the great mountains, then beyond the Ohio, the Allegheny and the Conewango; and now we are here on the borders of the great lakes, and a further push will throw me and my people off the log. If I ask, where is our land? a bird whispers in my ear, the Great King over the water has made peace with WASHINGTON and the thirteen fires, and divided the land between them by a line through the great lakes. Our Chiefs were not at the council, we were not warmed by its fire, nor protected by its heat. Our ally, in his hurry to make peace, forgot his red brethren; and did not even invite them to smoke the calamut which he had prepared for the thirteen fires which had rebelled against him." The Chief, in conclusion, with a sad and anxious countenance, asked the question, "Where are we to go?" The only response

---

* The Indian name of the Governors of New York.

† The Indian name of William Penn; and subsequently applied to the Governors of Pennsylvania.

that was made was the sighing of the wind through the leaves of the forest. The traveler was silent.*

I have seen a large medal of WASHINGTON, on one side of which is his bust in armor facing to the right. On the reverse or opposite side, is a full length figure of an Indian chief looking to the left, with an arrow in his right hand, and leaning on a bow; it contains the inscription "*The land was ours.*" It also inscribes to WASHINGTON these words: "*Innumerable millions yet unborn will venerate the memory of the man who obtained their country's freedom.*" Both these inscriptions command our assent. It thus appears that what was partial evil to the red man may be regarded as universal good to the human race. The former gives way to the advancing column of civilization, and will disappear from the land unless he abandons the life of a wanderer, and acquires a fixed home, where he can cultivate the soil and pursue the arts of civilized industry.

It would be inappropriate to this occasion, to enter upon a discussion of the causes of the gradual disappearance of the Indian race, when coming in contact with white men, nor of the tendency of the intercourse between these races of men to deteriorate the former and reduce their numbers. Neither can I enter upon the ethics involved in such a discussion. I leave these topics to the moral philosopher and the historian.

The distinguished Chief whose memory we this day commemorate, met these questions as practical facts. CORNPLANTER had learned from observation as well as

---

* Rev. SAMUEL KIRTLAND, missionary among the Indians, was the traveler referred to. He stated the substance of this anecdote to my father, Rev. NATHANIEL R. SNOWDEN.

experience, the influence and power of the whites, and as an able statesmen and friend of his race, he yielded to the superior force, and endeavored to preserve the existence of his family and nation, by securing for his people, land and other property where they would not be disturbed by the encroachment of the whites. It is a noticeable fact, and highly illustrative of his far-seeing policy, that in the treaties in which he took part as a Chief or representative of his tribe, he declined to stipulate for, or receive money or goods, but asked for well defined boundaries to their territories, or for land by title in fee simple to himself and to his people. He had the sagacity to perceive that if his nation and people depended upon a mere hunter's right to roam over a section of country, they would be driven, like other Indian tribes, from place to place, and at length be either exterminated or removed to distant lands, where they would be regarded as new comers, and be oppressed or destroyed by the Indians who had a prior claim to the territory.

Before making further remarks upon the life, character and public services of CORNPLANTER, I deem it proper to present some general observations respecting the Indian League or Confederacy,* known originally as the Five Nations, called by the French, Iroquois, and afterwards as the Six Nations, of which the tribe of CORNPLANTER, the Senecas,† was the most numerous and powerful. The Confederacy was originally composed of the

---

* Ho-do-no-sau-nee, or the United People.

† The original name of this tribe was Nun-da-wa-o-no, which means Great Hill People. The modern name is a corruption of a Dutch word for vermillion, *Sinnekar*, and has reference to the fact, that this tribe, being the most warlike of the Six Nations, used the war paint more than the others.

Senecas, Oneidas, Mohawks, Onondagos and Cayugas. To these were added in the year 1712, the Tuscaroras, who had previously resided, and had their hunting ground in North Carolina, but in that year were driven north by the southern Indians, and were added to the League, thence afterwards called the Six Nations. In many authorities and manuscripts, however, they continued to be denominated the Five Nations.

The power and influence of this Confederacy of nations, or Iroquois, at the time when the emigrants from Europe set their feet upon the extensive country, now embraced in the States of New York and Pennsylvania, and the extensive region beyond the Ohio, even to the Mississippi, were great; and overshadowed, if they did not actually control and govern, all other tribes of Indians within what is at the present time a large portion of the United States.

Their power even extended to the New England colonies and to Virginia. In 1684 the Governors of New York, Massachusetts and Virginia, met in council with the representative Chiefs of the Five Nations at Albany, "to strengthen and burnish," so says the treaty, "the covenant chain, and plant the tree of peace, of which the top should reach the sun, and the branches shelter the wide land." This treaty related not only to the territory in the actual possession of the Iroquois—called by them "The Long House," but embraced the extensive country from the St. Croix to the Albemarle. It may be interesting here, in order to illustrate the extent of their claims and authority, to quote a few words from the journal of Messrs. MASON and DIXON, when running their famous line. One of the original manuscript copies of which is in possession of the Historical Society of Pennsylvania. It is understood that there were three copies, in manuscript, prepared by these celebrated surveyors. I quote the following entries from the manuscript journal: "July 16, 1767. This day we were joined by fourteen Indians, deputed by the Chief of the Six Nations, to go with us on the line. With them came Mr. Hugh Crawford, interpreter." "October 9, 1767.—Crossed a war path near Dunkard creek. This day the Chief of the Indians, which joined us on the 16th July, informed us that the above mentioned war path was the extent of his commission from the Chief of the Six Nations, that he should go with us with the line; and that *he would not proceed one step farther.*"

Their principal seats, however, were in Western New York and North-western Pennsylvania. They were thus situated between the advancing column of emigration and settlements of the English from the Hudson, the Delaware, the Susquehanna and the Potomac on the one hand, and the French from Canada, the St. Lawrence, and the great lakes on the other. A territorial position, alike perilous to their aboriginal habits, customs and means of subsistence, as to their existence as a free and independent nation. And yet, notwithstanding these adverse circumstances, they stood for nearly two centuries, with an unshaken front, against the devastations of war, the blighting influence of foreign intercourse, and the still more fatal encroachments of a restless and advancing border population. United under their federal system, they maintained their independence and their power of self-protection long after the New England and Virginia races had surrendered their jurisdiction and fallen into the condition of conquered and dependent nations. And they now stand forth upon the canvas of Indian history prominent alike for the wisdom of their civil institutions, their sagacity in the administration of the affairs of the League and their courage in its defence. (Morgan's League of the Iroquois.)

Their system of government was remarkable for its simplicity and strength. The separate tribes, though united in one council fire, which was usually kindled and kept burning at Onandago, were, to some extent, sovereign and independent. In fact, their government was somewhat similar in structure to that which is established in the United States. Several republics were embraced in one. There were Chiefs for each tribe. Hereditary to a qualified extent, but dependent upon a ceremony of confirmation or investiture. Sometimes merit and public confidence would induce this investiture, without regard to hereditary right.

Sir WILLIAM JOHNSTON states, "that the Sachems of each tribe of the Six Nations were annually chosen in a public assembly of the Chiefs and Warriors, whenever a vacancy happened by death or otherwise. They were selected from among the oldest Warriors, for their sense and bravery, and approved of by all the tribe, after which they were selected as Sachems. Military services were the chief recommendations to this rank; but in some instances, a kind of inheritance in the office was recognized." I think there was a distinction between the *Sachems* and the *Chiefs*. The former had the direction of civil affairs and government, and the latter led the tribes in war. The rank of Sachem was in general hereditary, whilst that of Chief was conferred on account of ability, and especially bravery in war. A certain number of Chiefs were assigned to the different tribes. These Chiefs formed the council of the League, and in them was lodged the executive, legislative and judicial authority, for the general purposes of the united nations. As illustrative of the character of their government, I here insert the address of the Six Nations, to the colonies of Pennsylvania, Virginia and Maryland, delivered at the treaty made in Lancaster, Pennsylvania, in 1744. " We heartily recommend union and agreement between you, our brethren. Never disagree, but preserve a strict friendship for one another, and thereby you, as well as we, will become the stronger. Our wise forefathers established amity and friendship among the Five Nations. This has made us formidable, and has given us weight and authority with the neighboring nations. We are a powerful Confederacy, and by your observing the same means which our wise forefathers pursued, you will acquire fresh strength and power. Therefore whatever befalls you, never fall out with one another."

These are memorable words, and indicate the complacency of the members of the Confederacy with their own condition and power. Feeling secure in their castles beyond the mountains, and contented with their homes, amidst their beautiful lakes, and rivers and forests, where they possessed towns and villages, cultivated fields and orchards of various fruits, and being kindly disposed to their white brethren of the English colonies, they ventured the friendly task of giving them such wise and excellent counsel and advice, as is worthy of being re-produced on this occasion, although one hundred and twenty-two years have passed away since its delivery on the banks of the Conestoga.

Governor DE WITT CLINTON, in his address before the Historical Society of New York, December 6, 1811, quotes the foregoing address, and says: "This ancient and cementing principle of union and fraternity, which has connected them in friendship, and which was the basis of their power, and the pillar of their greatness, has been entirely driven from them. Party, in all its forms and violence, rages among them with uncontrolled sway. The nations are split up into fragments; the son is arrayed against the father; brother against brother; families against families; tribes against tribes. They are divided into factions—religious, political and personal; Christian and Pagan; American and British—the followers of CORNPLANTER and RED JACKET, of Skonadoi and Captain PETER. The minister of destruction is hovering over them; and before the passing away of the present generation, not a single Iroquois will be seen in this State."

This sad picture, although true to some extent, was somewhat overdrawn in consequence of the agitation and disputes which preceded the war with England in 1812; the Indian tribes being divided upon that question, some of them taking up the hatchet for England, and others, among whom were the Six Nations, for the United States. But Gov. DE WITT CLINTON'S *prophecy* has utterly failed. The influence and example of CORNPLANTER, assisted by other good men, white as well as red, leading their people to agriculture, and to habits of industry and temperance, has saved from destruction a remnant of the brave and once powerful nations, who lived on these rivers and lakes, and possessed the land, both far and near.

Here, at the grave of the venerated CORNPLANTER, we can see the results of his principles, his measures and example. Here he rests from his labors, but his works do follow him. I see this in the evidences of civilization, industry and competency around me. I see it in the countenances of these intelligent and respectable people of the Indian race, who are endeavoring to imitate his example, and who come here this day to do honor to his immortal memory.

The Indian name of the venerable Chief, to whose memory this monument is erected, is written in different manners, in publication documents and papers, which have come under my notice. At the treaty of Fort Harmer, his name was given thus: "Gy-ant-wa-chi-a;" and this orthography I prefer. It means The Planter. But it is, also, elsewhere written, "Gy-ant-wa-hia," and in this form it appears on this monument; also "Ki-on-twog-ky," "Gy-ant-wa-ka," "Ki-end-twoh-ke," and "Cy-ent-wo-kee." In Mr. DAY's historical collection of Pennsylvania, and Mr. STONE's Life of RED JACKET, and in some other modern works, he is named, "Ga-nio-di-euh," or "Handsome Lake;" but this is an error. That was the name of a half-brother of our Chief, who was also designated as the prophet, to whom I shall hereafter have occasion to refer. Our Chief was frequently designated as Captain O'BAIL, or ABEEL, (Captain being the highest military distinction known to the Indians;) but he was generally named and best known as CORNPLANTER or THE CORNPLANTER.

He was born at Ganowaugus, otherwise written Conewaugus, an important town of the Seneca Indians, situated on the Genessee river, and on the trail or main road through the country of the Six Nations, to Niagara.

We have no precise knowledge of the date of his birth. He has been heard to say, that he and General WASHINGTON were about the same age. This would place his birth in the year 1732. In 1831, THOMAS STRUTHERS, Esq., of Warren, visited CORNPLANTER at his house, in this town, on which occasion the Chief, in answer to the question, "How old are you?" replied, "One hundred years." I saw him in the summer of 1834. At my interview with him, Mr. GEORGE POWERS, of Franklin, Venango county, acted as interpreter. On that occasion he said he was more than one hundred years of age. A learned writer,* speaking of a younger brother of CORNPLANTER, named "Gancodiyo, or Handsome Lake," says "he was born at the Indian village of Ga-no-wau-ges, near Avon, about the year 1735." He was a half-brother of our hero, having the same *mother*. Mr. THATCHER, in his Indian biography, and some other writers, have fallen into the gross error of making their relationship through a common *father*. I refer, in this connection, to the statement of the time of the birth of "Handsome Lake," in conjunction with the other facts mentioned, as corroborative of the probability, that the subject of these remarks was born about the year 1732.

At that period, the trade with the Six Nations was chiefly in the hands of the English. One of their principal traders was JOHN ABEEL,† generally named O'BAIL

---

* Mr. MORGAN.

† I have recently been informed that JOHN ABEEL, the father of CORNPLANTER, was a Hollander or Dutchman. The inaccurate way of writing the name O'BAIL, has given rise to the statement, generally believed, that he was of a different nation. I learn that CORNPLANTER visited a nephew of JOHN ABEEL, who resided in the city of New York, and their relationship was recognized. I have this information from a great-grand-son

or O'BEEL; his name is mentioned in the annals of that period on several occasions. At one time it is stated, that he made presents of considerable value to the Indians. It was one of the hospitable customs of these people, to give their friends a wife. JOHN ABEEL had his Indian squaw, and CORNPLANTER was the fruit of that temporary union. Although we have no certain information on the subject, I think it probable that the mother was the daughter of an Indian Sachem. I infer this from the fact, that the best and most respectable traders of that period, were regarded with great favor by the Indians, and also from the important circumstance, that three of her sons were recognized as Chiefs of the Seneca tribe, namely: her celebrated son, CORNPLANTER, and her younger sons, Ga-ne-o-di-yo, or Handsome Lake, and Ta-wau-ne-ars, or Blacksnake.

We may also reasonably infer that she faithfully and carefully discharged her duty to her offspring, in accordance with the light and knowledge which she possessed. It was the Indian woman who planted the fields of corn, and kept the wigwam, when the hunter was in the forest, or the warrior was upon the war path. Their attachment to localities was greater than that of the Indian men. It sometimes happened that Indian women interposed to prevent grant of lands by the chiefs and warriors. They desired to preserve their wigwams, their fields and their orchards. The father of CORNPLANTER being absent, chiefly residing at Albany, or on the Mohawk river, the mother's influence was uncontrolled. I

---

of the nephew referred to. The original manner of writing the name was ABEEL. The family now write it ABEEL. I regret that the name is inaccurately engraved on the monument erected at Jennesadaga.

think it highly probable that the remarkable attachment to the *land*, exhibited by CORNPLANTER on all occasions, was the result, in some good degree, of the teachings of his mother. When he speaks at the treaties, or sends a "talk" or a message to the Chief of the thirteen fires, or to "Corlear," (New York,) or to "Onas," (Pennsylvania,) he says: "We do not want money or goods; we want homes; we want land; the trader's goods soon wear out, the land lasts forever."

CORNPLANTER refers to his birth and childhood in his interesting address to the Governor of Pennsylvania, in 1822, when the question of taxing his property, hereinafter mentioned, was raised.

"I feel it my duty to send a speech to the Governor of Pennsylvania at this time, and inform him the place where I was from; which was *Connewaugus*, on the Genessee river.

"When I was a child, I played with the butterfly, the grasshopper and the frogs. As I grew up, I began to pay some attention and play with the Indian boys in the neighborhood, and they took notice of my skin being of a different color from theirs, and spoke about it. I inquired of my mother the cause, and she told me that my father was a resident of Albany. I still ate my victuals out of a bark dish—I grew up to be a young man, and married me a wife—but I had no kettle or gun. I then knew where my father lived and went to see him, and found he was a white man and spoke the English language."*

The period when CORNPLANTER and his family removed from Connewaugus and the Genessee country is

---

* Journal House of Representatives of Pennsylvania, 1822-23.

unknown. Probably not until his native town was destroyed by General SULLIVAN, in his expedition against the Six Nations, in 1779. Of that expedition, CORNPLANTER speaks in his address to General WASHINGTON in 1790. From the strong and eloquent language used by him, and which I shall have occasion hereafter to cite, it is probable he was an eye witness of the desolation produced by SULLIVAN's army.

Of the early career of CORNPLANTER, we have but little information. It is generally understood that his first appearance as a warrior, was at the battle of the Monougahela, in 1755, where BRADDOCK was defeated, and that he fought on the side of the French in that bloody field.

A word here explanatory of the position of the Senecas, and their relations with the Indians of the League, and other neighboring nations, may be useful. The Seneca tribe was more exposed to the French and their Indian allies on the lower Ohio and the lakes, than the other members of the League. They had the important and dangerous duties of keeping "the western door of the long house," as they termed their possessions. Their watch and ward extended from the Susquehanna to the Ohio and great lakes. The duplicity, and in fact treachery of the English crown, during the reign of the STUARTS, in not only abandoning the Six Nations in their war with the French which they had undertaken in the interest of the English, but when the League had defeated the French and well-nigh conquered them, the English government compelled them to make peace with France, and submit to the terms which the French dictated. These terms, however, could not concede to the

French a region of country from which they had been expelled, and which was in fact occupied by the Six Nations; and thus the whole country, south of the chain of the great lakes, was rescued from Canada. Referring to this period, Mr. BANCROFT says: "In the course of events, New York owes its present northern boundary to the valor of the Five Nations. But for them, Canada would have embraced the basin of the St. Lawrence."* Although the Six Nations were afterwards informed that the treachery and duplicity herein referred to, was not approved by the successors of the STUARTS, nor by the English people, but was the result of the bad conduct of English kings who were under French influence, yet it left an impression on their minds which had an injurious effect in after years.

By the regulations of the League, in cases where the United Council did not act authoritatively for the whole Confederacy, it appears that the separate tribes were not precluded from engaging in war; nor individual warriors prevented from taking up the hatchet, as inclination might lead them. Acting under these principles, some of the Six Nations fought on the side of the French, during the war of 1755 and 1762, including that part of the Senecas who had their seat north of the Ohio, and below Fort Duquesne; and some on the upper Ohio, now called Allegheny, united with them. From these considerations it is not at all improbable that CORNPLANTER, then a warrior of twenty-three years of age, was on the war path at BRADDOCK's defeat. It was probably his first battle, as it was also the first in which our WASHINGTON was engaged. The Indians of the

---
* History United States, volume II, page 424.

Ohio and the lakes were, at this period, more apprehensive of the encroachments of the Virginians and the English generally, than of the French. The former were accompanied by the land surveyor and the woodman's axe ;* the latter had in their train only the engineer to build forts, and a commissariat which supplied the wants of the Indians, as well as their own. Hence, a portion of the Senecas, of the upper Ohio, were induced to take the side of the French. CORNPLANTER, with a portion of his tribe, probably formed a part of that martial array which we are told set forth from Fort Venango, at the mouth of Venango river, now called French creek, (Franklin, Pennsylvania,) for the forks of the Ohio, embarked in three hundred canoes and batteaux, and having eighteen pieces of cannon.

The French war closed in the year 1763, by the treaty of UTRECHT. The Indian tribes were at peace with each other and with their white neighbors. It was about this time that CORNPLANTER married a wife, an Indian woman of his own tribe. When that important event took place, he, himself, informs us, that he was not well provided for housekeeping. He "had no gun, and his wife no kettle." Under the impression that his father would provide these useful articles for him, he made a journey to Albany, to see him. But he was disappointed. In CORNPLANTER's own account of the interview, he

---

* A few years later than this period the Virginians made great encroachments upon the boundary of the Indians. Lord DUNMORE and others, claimed large bodies of land north of the Ohio. The Indians, for a long period of time, claimed that the Ohio was the boundary between them and the whites. In 1773 Lord DUNMORE caused surveys to be made at the Falls of the Ohio; and lands in that region are now held under his warrants and surveys.

says: "When I started home my father gave me no provision to eat on the way. He gave me neither kettle nor gun. Neither did he tell me that the United States were about to rebel against the government of England." This conduct was alike unnatural and unjust. For, if the result of the French war had impoverished the Indian trader, of which we have no knowledge, he, at least, might have given his son some information of the dark clouds which were beginning to gather between England and the colonies, and which soon afterwards brought on the Revolutionary war. CORNPLANTER, in the address just referred to, intimates that it was a want of knowledge of the questions in dispute, in conjunction with other causes which he mentions in his address to WASHINGTON, in 1790, led the Confederacy to take part, in favor of the King of England, in the war which ensued.

He says, in the address referred to, he was opposed to joining in the conflict, inasmuch as the Indians had nothing to do with the difficulties that existed between the two parties. If he had more clearly understood the points in dispute his opposition might have been more effective. When BRANT, early in the year 1777, with his Mohawks, had organized a hostile expedition, in connection with some loyalists of that region, to attack Unadillo, in New York, on the Upper Susquehanna, an embassy of Sachems and war Chiefs of the Senecas and Cayugas repaired to Oghwago, to which place BRANT had advanced, to remonstrate with him against further hostilities to the Americans. BRANT yielded to their councils and protestations, and withdrew, with his Indians and refugees, into the Cayuga country. BRANT'S exertions and interference had much to do in inducing the Six Nations to take part against the united colonies. Not long after the above occurrence, in an interview with General HERKIMER, of the Revolutionary army, he said: "The Indians were in concert with their King, as their fathers had been. The King's belts, of Wampum, are yet lodged with them, and they cannot violate their pledges. General HERKIMER and his followers have joined the Boston people against their sovereign. And, although the Boston people were resolute, yet the King would humble them. That General SCHUYLER was very smart on the Indians, at the treaty of German Flats, but, at the same time, was not able to afford the smallest article of clothing; and finally, that the Indians had formerly made war on the white people, when they were all united, and as they were now divided the Indians were not frightened."*

But when the representative Chiefs of the Confederacy at Oswego, at a general council held in the summer of 1777, decided to take up the hatchet for the King of England, CORNPLANTER and his tribe considered themselves bound by the decision. His nation was at war, and he had to be at war. As the boys say at school, "when you are in Rome, you must do as Rome does." In his address to WASHINGTON, at Philadelphia, in 1790, he justifies, or at least palliates the conduct of his nation in taking the side of the King, in the following eloquent and impressive words: "Father, when you kindled your thirteen fires separately, the wise men assembled at them told us you were all brothers—the children of one great

---

* STONE'S life of BRANT, quoting from the Herkimer papers and annals of Tryon county.

Father, who regarded the red people as his children. They called us brothers, and invited us to their protection. They told us that he resided beyond the great water, where the sun first rises, and that he was a King, whose power no people could resist, and that his goodness was as bright as the sun. What they said went to our hearts. We accepted the invitation and promised to obey him. What the Seneca nation promise, they faithfully perform. When you refused obedience to that King, he commanded us to assist his beloved men in making you sober. In obeying him, we did no more than yourselves had led us to promise. We were deceived; but your people teaching us to confide in that King, had helped to deceive us, and we now appeal to your heart. Is all the blame ours?"

In addition to these considerations, thus cautiously presented by CORNPLANTER, it is well known that the hostilities commenced on the north-western frontier of Virginia, by the cruel and unprovoked war waged against the Indians by the land-jobbers, under the direction of the notorious Captain MICHAEL CRESAP, had a decided effect upon the Six Nations, in determining on which side they would take in the conflict which soon followed. The attrocious murder of the family of LOGAN, by CRESAP, is well known, and need not be repeated on this occasion. LOGAN was the son of SHIKELLIMUS, a distinguished Cayuga Sachem. JAMES LOGAN, an eminent member of the Colonial Council of Pennsylvania, was the friend of SHIKELLIMUS; the Sachem had named his son for Mr. LOGAN. CONRAD WEISER, the well known Indian agent and interpreter, writing from Tulpehocken, in Berks county, under date of July 6, 1747. to Secretary

Peters, says: "Shikellimus gives his respects to his old friend, Mr. Logan. He intends to see him in Philadelphia before next fall."* Shikellimus had been sent by the Six Nations to preside over and govern the Delawares, Shawanees, Conoys, Nantikokes, Monseys and Mohicans. This interesting fact shows the superior power and authority of the Six Nations, and that these tribes were subordinate to them. Shikellimus resided at Shamokin, a large Indian village near the junction of the North and West Branches of the Susquehanna river, the site of the present borough of Sunbury, in Northumberland county, Pennsylvania. This memorable Sachem governed these tribes with ability and integrity, for a great many years.

Logan had a temporary residence on Kishicokelas creek, a beautiful limestone spring, a mile or two above the wild gorge where the creek passes Jack's mountain, (now in Mifflin county, Pennsylvania.) Here he lived several years. This was before the year 1768, when, by the treaty of Fort Stanwix, the Indians relinquished to the proprietary government all that region of country. He then moved with his family to the country beyond the Ohio, and fixed his cabin below Wheeling, where, a few years later, his whole family were barbarously murdered. On the Sciota, in 1774, he delivered his well known speech to Lord Dunmore, first published in Mr. Jefferson's notes on Virginia. A careful historian, Mr. Day, says: "That it is now well authenticated that Logan, himself, composed the speech, and that the common supposition, that Mr. Jefferson was the author of it, is an error."

---
* Colonial Records of Pennsylvania.

It is well known that LOGAN, born at Shamokin, where the Moravians had a missionary station, received some rudimental education from them, and was baptized; his father, SHIKELLIMUS, giving him the name LOGAN, after his friend JAMES LOGAN, the Secretary of the Province. LOGAN's speech, on the occasion referred to, though often published, I insert here. It was as follows: "I appeal to any white man to say, if ever he entered LOGAN's cabin hungry, and he gave him not meat; if ever he came naked, and he clothed him not. During the course of the last long and bloody war, LOGAN remained idle in his cabin, an advocate for peace. Such was my love for the whites that my countrymen pointed, as they passed, and said, 'LOGAN is the friend of white men.' I had even thought to have lived with you, but for the injuries of one man, Colonel CRESAP, the last spring in cold blood, and unprovoked, murdered all the relations of LOGAN, not even sparing my women and children. There runs not a drop of my blood in the veins of any living creature. This called on me for revenge. I have sought it. I have killed many. I have fully glutted my vengeance. For my country I rejoice at the beams of peace. But do not harbor a thought that mine is the joy of fear. LOGAN never felt fear. He will not turn his heel to save his life. Who is there to mourn for LOGAN? Not one."

The cruel murder of the family of LOGAN, (himself a distinguished Chief, and the friend of the whites and of peace,) made a deep impression upon the Six Nations, and was probably one of the causes which induced them to take up the hatchet for the King of England. The final decision, as already stated, was made at Oswego, where the representative Chiefs and warriors were assembled, being drawn thither by the united exertions of Sir JOHN JOHNSTON and Colonel JOHN BUTLER, aided by BRANT, the indefatigible and bitter enemy of the united colonies. The British commissioners promised the Indians an ample reward if they would assist the English to subdue the rebel colonies. The Chiefs, in reply, stated that they were bound, by the treaties at Germon Flats and Albany, to be neutral to the war. Their objections, however, were overcome, by the commissioners telling them, " that the people of the colonies were few in number, and would be easily subdued; and that, on account of their disobedience to the King, they justly merited all the punishment that it was possible for white men and Indians to inflict upon them." " The King," they said, " was rich and powerful, both in money and subjects. His rum was as plenty as the water in Lake Ontario, and his men as numerous as the sands upon its shore. And the Indians were assured that if they would assist in the war, and persevere in their friendship for the King, until its close, they should never want for goods or money." Overcome by these importunities, and by a recital of the injuries they had received from some of the people of the colonies, aided by a display of a large quantity of trinkets, blankets, clothes, guns, and other articles and implements, the Indians concluded a treaty of alliance with Great Britain, and took up the hatchet against the united colonies. At the close of the treaty, each Indian was presented with a suit of clothes, a brass kettle, a gun, a tomahawk and scalping knife, a quantity of ammunition and a piece of gold. MARY JEMISON, from whom we quote this statement, says, "as late as 1823, the brass kettles received at Oswego, were in use by the Senecas." Here CORNPLANTER, no doubt, secured the "gun and kettle" which he had, in vain, expected from his father. And the contrast between these munificent gifts, and the fact stated by BRANT, that General SCHUYLER, at the treaty of German Flats, was not able to afford to the Indians the smallest article of clothing, no doubt assisted to turn the scale in favor of the King.

During the military operations which followed this important transaction, CORNPLANTER fought against the United States. It is said that he was in the bloody battle of Wyoming, which occurred on the 3d of July, 1778. It is considered to be a doubtful point, whether the celebrated BRANT was in that battle. There is high poetical authority* in favor of it, and some corroborative evidence of the fact. But there is no evidence that has come under my notice, that CORNPLANTER was present.

CORNPLANTER was with his tribe, in endeavoring to resist the advance of General SULLIVAN into the country of the Six Nations, in the year 1779. He was present and took part in the battle of New Town, the present site of Elmira, New York, where the Indians and British troops, the latter under the command of Colonel JOHN BUTLER, were signally defeated. CORNPLANTER and RED JACKET were with the Senecas. We do not know which of these Chiefs had the immediate command of the warriors of that tribe. It is known, however, that BRANT, who had by general consent a superior authority, charged RED JACKET with being the principal

---

* CAMPBELL'S Gertrude of Wyoming.

cause of the disaster of that day, and said that although he was a great orator, he was no warrior; on the contrary, he was a coward. In a council held some years afterwards, CORNPLANTER made a similar charge against RED JACKET, to which the latter replied, "I am an orator—I was born an orator."

This decisive action on the Chemung, was followed by the devastation of the Indian towns and settlements throughout the country of the Senecas and Cayugas. They had several towns and many large villages laid out with a considerable degree of regularity. They had framed houses, some of them well finished, and painted and having chimneys. They had broad and productive fields, and in addition to abundance of apples, they had orchards of peaches, pears and plums. But after the battle of New Town, terror led the van of the invader, whose approach was heralded by watchmen stationed upon every height, and desolation followed weeping in his train. The Indians every where fled, as SULLIVAN advanced, and the whole country was swept as with the besom of destruction. Towns were burned, fields laid waste, cattle destroyed and the orchards cut down.* CORNPLANTER was a sad witness to the destruction of his own home and village, and that of his people. He refers to these scenes most eloquently, in his address to WASHINGTON, in 1792. "When your army entered the country of the Six Nations, we called you the "town destroyer;" and to this day, when that name is heard, our women look behind them, and turn pale, and our children cling close to the necks of their mothers. Our

---

* STONE in his Life of BRANT.

councillors and warriors are men, and cannot be afraid, but their hearts are grieved with the fears of women and children."

This expedition of General SULLIVAN'S, was followed by numerous retaliations by the Indians. The most prominent of which was the invasion of Schoharie and its destruction, together with the towns and settlements in the valley of the Mohawk. Whilst Sir JOHN JOHNSTON and BRANT had the principal command, CORNPLANTER led his tribe in this invasion, and was in the battle of Klock's Field, on the Mohawk river; the result of which was a decided check upon the Indians and their allies, and compelled them to fall back to Oswego.

The residence of JOHN ABEEL, the father of CORNPLANTER, was in the vicinity of the recent battle ground. Before retiring with his warriors, CORNPLANTER made a detour in the direction of his father's residence, and took him prisoner. After taking him a few miles into the forest, he made to him the following address: "My name is JOHN ABEEL, commonly called CORNPLANTER. I am your son. You are my father. You are my prisoner, and subject to the customs of Indian warfare. But you shall not be harmed. You need not fear. I am a warrior. Many are the scalps I have taken. I am your son. I was anxious to see you, and greet you in friendship. I went to your cabin and took you by force; but your life shall be spared. Indians love their friends and their kindred, and treat them with kindness. If you choose to follow the fortunes of your red son, and live with our people, I will cherish your old age with plenty of venison, and you shall live easy. But if it is your choice to return to your friends, and live with your white children.

I will send a party of my trusty young men to conduct you back in safety. I respect you, my father. You have been friendly to Indians. They are your friends." This address shews the magnanimity of CORNPLANTER, and that he could forget his father's neglect to supply him with a "gun and kettle," on the occasion hereinbefore mentioned. The elder ABEEL declined the offer. His son fulfilled his word, and gave his father a suitable escort. He returned to his dwelling in safety. The proud Seneca and his warriors moved off to their own wilds.* These events transpired in 1780. Of the subsequent military career of CORNPLANTER, little is known. He probably participated in the skirmishes and expeditions during the subsequent years of the Revolutionary war and until its close. He never spoke in after life of his career as a Chief or warrior; and history gives us no details of these expeditions and skirmishes, except as to the second invasion of the Mohawk valley, and the battle of Durlagh, in 1781, in which there is no mention of CORNPLANTER being present.

The United States successfully maintained by the sword the principles announced on the 4th of July, 1776, at Philadelphia; and England, at the close of the war in 1783, acknowledged their independence. From that period CORNPLANTER became the friend of the United States, and the uniform and consistent advocate for peace.

---

* This anecdote is related in MARY JAMISON'S narrative, and is cited by Mr. STONE, in his interesting life of BRANT, wherein the author says "In every instance in which he has had an opportunity of testing by other authorities, the correctness of MARY JAMISON'S statement, they have proved to be remarkably correct." Mr. STONE adds: "CORNPLANTER was an able man, distinguished in subsequent negotiations; he was an eloquent orator and a great advocate for temperance."

He put forth, on all occasions, his best efforts to secure the friendship of the United States, and to preserve his nation from the destruction which seemed so eminently impending. England, in her treaty of peace, made no provision for her allies of the Six Nations. Many of the Chiefs of the latter were disposed to make common cause with the other Indians of the continent, and continue the war. But the sagacious mind of CORNPLANTER led him to the just conclusion, that a continuance of the war would be the destruction of his nation and tribe. He was the chief instrument in effecting the treaty of peace at Fort Stanwix, in 1784.

There had been a former treaty at Fort Stanwix, namely: on the 5th of November, 1768, between the Proprietors of Pennsylvania and the Chief of the Six Nations. The territory granted to Pennsylvania, is particularly described in the second volume of SMITH's Laws of Pennsylvania, page 122–3. At the second treaty of Fort Stanwix, held in October, 1784, the Pennsylvania commissioners inquired what creek was meant by Tiadaghton, also the Indian name of Burnett's hills, which was left blank in the deed of 1768. The Indians then said that Tiadaghton, is the same creek which the whites called Pine creek, (now in Lycoming county.) As to Burnett's hills, they called them the "Long mountains," and knew them by no other name. The boundaries established by the treaty of October 23, 1784, made the said Pine creek the line, and down the same to its mouth, on the West Branch of the Susquehanna; thence up the south side thereof to the fork of the same river, which lies nearer to a place on the Ohio river, (Allegheny,) called Kittanning, and from the fork by a straight line to Kittanning, and thence down the said river Ohio, to where the western bounds of Pennsylvania crosses the same river.

CORNPLANTER " very well knew," says Mr. STONE, in his life of RED JACKET, " that by assenting to the large cessions of territory exacted by the treaty, he was jeopardizing his popularity with his people. But if others had not, he had the sagacity to perceive, that although he and his people had served the crown of Great Britain with all fidelity, they had nevertheless been abandoned to their fate by their more powerful ally, and the alternative was presented to them of giving up as much of their territory as the United States demanded, or of yielding the whole of it. His course, and it was also the course of wisdom, was prescribed by the necessity of the case, and by the energy and ability with which he conducted the negotiation, he yet retained for his people an ample and beautiful territory. He was the most prominent Indian Chief in the treaty of Fort Harmer, in 1789.

By this treaty other grants of land were made. The cession of the Presque Isle lands, is dated January 9, 1789, in which the signing Chiefs acknowledge the right of soil and jurisdiction over that tract of country, ceded by New York and Massachusetts, on the margin of Lake Erie, including Presque Isle, and the bays and harbors above the margin of Lake Erie. This territory was afterwards, namely, on the 13th of April, 1791, purchased from the United States, by the State of Pennsylvania, for the consideration of $151,640 25, paid in Continental certificates of various descriptions.

CORNPLANTER was present as a prominent Chief, at the treaty held with the Indians, in Marietta, Ohio, in the year 1789. On this occasion, an elegant entertainment was provided. The utmost satisfaction appeared to prevail among all the parties to the treaty. Good wine was served after the dinner, and CORNPLANTER being called on for a toast, took up a glass and said: "I thank the Great Spirit for this opportunity of smoking the pipe of friendship and love. May we plant our own vines, be the fathers of our own children, and maintain them."

The services of CORNPLANTER on this, and other occasions, were highly appreciated by the Ohio Land Company. This company was formed in 1786, by officers of the army of the Revolution. At the close of the war of 1783, the officers and soldiers were paid in Loan Office certificates, worth, in specie, about 2s. 6d. in the £. On the 16th June, 1783, a large number of them, with the approval of WASHINGTON, memorialized Congress for lands to settle on north-west of the Ohio river. The action of the Government in this matter does not very clearly appear, although it seems that the officers of the Treasury recognized the validity of an arrangement to receive loan certificates in payment for the land. In 1786, the Ohio company was organized, and by their agents contracted with the Government for 1,500,000 acres of land, in the North-Western territory, for $1,000,000, in Loan Office certificates, reduced to specie value.

At a meeting of the directors and agents of the company, held at Campus Martius, (Marietta,) Ohio, February 9, 1789, the following proceedings were had:

"*Whereas*, GYANTWACHIA, or THE CORNPLANTER, a Chief of the Seneca nation, has since the treaty of peace, made in the year 1784, between the United States and the Indian nations, in many instances, been of great service to the United States; and the friendship he has manifested to the proprietors of land purchased by the Ohio company, has been of particular service to them; therefore,

Resolved, That one mile square of the donation lands be granted to GYANTWACHIA, and his heirs forever, in such place as the committee appointed to examine proper places of settlement shall assign; and that the duties, conditions and limitations required of other settlers on such land, shall in this grant be dispensed with. And the said committee of five are directed to give him a deed accordingly."—[*Ohio Company Records, p.* 54.]

The above interesting transaction was communicated to me by W. S. WARD, Esq., of Marietta, Ohio. He says, however, that there is no evidence, so far as he can learn, that the committee or agents ever selected this "mile square," donated to CORNPLANTER; consequently he received no deed for the land. Probably there may be some documents on this subject among the papers of CORNPLANTER. The Chief always carefully preserved his important papers, and they are now in the hands of his decendants at Jennesedaga.

The grants of lands made at these treaties, gave offence to many of the Senecas and others of the Six Nations, led on by the opposition of RED JACKET and BRANT. He was not only vilified and misrepresented, but his life was even threatened. He resolved to present to *his* friend, and the friend of the human race, WASHINGTON, the condition of his nation and his own peril.

CORNPLANTER came to Philadelphia, by the way of

Fort Franklin and Fort Pitt, traveling with his party down the Allegheny river in canoes. At Fort Franklin, ensign JEFFERS, of the 1st Pennsylvania regiment, was in command. He furnished our Chief with a letter of recommendation, in which he says: "The bearer hereof, GYENTWOKEE, the head Chief of the Seneca nation, is an undoubted friend of the United States. When the Indians have stolen horses and other things from our people, I have known him, with the greatest dignity, to give orders for them to be returned. I never knew his orders to be disobeyed. When the people of Cussewago (now Meadville) were about to fly on account of unfavorable reports about some of the Southern (Western) Indians, he sent a speech to me, in which he said, 'he wished the people to keep their minds easy, and take care of the corn fields, that the Six Nations were friends; that should the Western Indians invade the settlements, he would gather his warriors and help to drive them to the setting of the sun.' In consequence of this, the people rested easy. On his arrival here, he told me that should I be invaded, so that I could not get provisions, that he and his warriors would clear the way; he said that at the Council at the Muskingum the great men asked him which side he would die on? He told them on the side of the Americans. He says he is of the same mind yet. Sundry other things might be said, but as he is now on his way to attend the Assembly at Philadelphia, I will only recommend him to the particular attention of the good people of Pennsylvania, between here and that place. They may depend upon it, that they not only entertain a friend, but a friend of great consequence, for the Seneca nation is so much governed by him, that if he says *war*, it is *war*; and if he says *peace*, it is *peace*. He is, therefore, a man worthy of the greatest attention. The other Chiefs with him, second him in every thing, and are men worthy of great attention."

This interesting letter was addressed "To the good people between here (Fort Franklin) and Philadelphia." It was of great service to CORNPLANTER on his journey; and when he arrived in Philadelphia, he placed it in the hands of Governor MIFFLIN. The paper is among the archives of Pennsylvania, and is endorsed "1790, recommendary letter from I. JEFFERS, ensign of the 1st Pennsylvania regiment, commanding Fort Franklin, on French creek, in favor of CYENTWOKEE, or CORNPLANTER." *

It appears that from Pittsburg to Philadelphia, CORNPLANTER and his party were accompanied by Mr. JOSEPH NICHOLSON, the interpreter. Dr. JOHN WILKINS, Sr., writes from Shippensburg, to Gov. MIFFLIN, under date October 14, 1790, as follows: "I have just met at this place, CORNPLANTER, and the other Indian Chiefs, invited by Council. The reasons they assign for being detained, are such as I hope will induce Council to exert themselves in doing every thing in their power to give them satisfaction. CORNPLANTER says when he was preparing to come down, agreeably to the invitation from Council, his nation was excited to great tumult, by the killing the two Chiefs, on Pine creek, and he was obliged to stay to pacify them. The Shawanese Indians, who are the most troublesome, sent a message to the Seneca nation, telling them, that unless they declared war against the white people, they should be cut off. This message had to be taken into consideration by a

* Pennsylvania Archives, 1790, p. 86.

general Council of the Nation, and this required time. The subject of this visit of the Chiefs of the Seneca nation is of great consequence to the people of the western country. The conductor and interpreter, Mr. JOSEPH NICHOLSON, has brought them thus far at his own expense, but his money being exhausted, I have advanced him a sum sufficient to pay his expenses to the city. I need not give you a character of the CORNPLANTER; his friendship for the people of Pennsylvania, his pacific temper and integrity are sufficiently known."*

He traveled to Philadelphia, then the seat of government of the United States, accompanied by his steadfast friends and Chiefs of his nation, HALF TOWN and BIG TREE. On the arrival of the Chiefs at Philadelphia, they had an official audience with the President, on which occasion CORNPLANTER made an eloquent and dignified address, and which called forth an appropriate reply from WASHINGTON. To WASHINGTON he said, referring to General SULLIVAN's destruction of the Seneca towns: "We called you the 'town destroyer,' but when you gave us peace, we called you father, because you promised to secure us in the possession of our lands. Do this, and so long as the lands shall remain, that beloved name shall live in the heart of every Seneca." He then gives a terse and clear statement of the means taken to induce the Six Nations to make such extensive grants of their lands—grants, he adds, "made at a time when you told us that we were in your hand, and that by closing it, you could crush us to nothing; and you demanded from us a great country as the price of that peace which you had offered us; as if our want of strength had de-

---

* Pennsylvania Archives, 1790, p. 321.

stroyed our rights." Referring to his own conduct and its effect upon his tribe, he uses the following eloquent and patriotic words: "Father, we will not conceal from you, that the Great God, and not man, has preserved THE CORNPLANTER from the hands of his nation. For they continually ask, where is the land which our children, and their children after them, are to lie down upon? You told us, say they, that the line drawn from Pennsylvania to Lake Ontario, would mark it forever on the east, and the line running from Buffalo creek to Pennsylvania, would mark it on the west, and we see that it is not so. You, first one and then another, comes and takes it away by order of that people, which you tell us promised to secure it to us. He is silent—for he has nothing to answer. When the sun goes down, he opens his heart before God; and earlier than the sun appears upon the hills, he gives thanks for his protection during the night; for he feels, that among men become desperate by their danger—it is God only that can preserve him. He loves peace and all that he has had in store, he has given to those who have been robbed by your people, lest they should plunder the innocent to re-pay themselves. The whole season which others have employed in providing for their families, he has spent in his endeavors to preserve peace. At this moment his wife and children are lying upon the ground, and in want of food. His heart is in pain for them, but he perceives that the Great Spirit will try his firmness in doing what is right."

WASHINGTON made an appropriate reply to this address, which he caused to be engrossed, and was signed by himself and by Mr. JEFFERSON, then Secretary of State.

and presented to CORNPLANTER. The Chief valued this document among his highest treasures. A lithographic copy of it has been prepared for this occasion, and I will annex to this address, a copy of it and of the speeches of CORNPLANTER made on that occasion. A single remark made by WASHINGTON, I here introduce. "The merits of CORNPLANTER, and his friendship for the United States, are well known to me, and shall not be forgotten."

When CORNPLANTER arrived in Philadelphia, WASHINGTON was absent at his seat in Virginia. In his absence, the Chief was cordially received by the President and members of the Executive Council of the State of Pennsylvania. In the *Colonial Records* of Pennsylvania, the following minutes appear:

"PHILADELPHIA, *Saturday, October* 23, 1790.

"Present—His Excellency THOMAS MIFFLIN, Esq., President. SAMUEL MILES, RICHARD WILLING, ZEBULON POTTS, AMOS GREGG and Lord BUTLER, Esquires. CORNPLANTER and five other Indian Chiefs were introduced to Council. The President informed them, that the Supreme Executive Council of Pennsylvania was happy to see them, and ready to hear what they had to say. The Chief then made a short address, and asked for further time to conclude what to say, which was granted."

Subsequently the Chief made a more extended speech, to which Governor MIFFLIN made an appropriate reply. Vol. XVI, p. 496.

WASHINGTON continued to be the friend of CORNPLANTER to the end of his public career, and this confidence and friendship afforded a source of consolation to the Chief, for the dissatisfaction of a portion of his tribe, led on by the crafty RED JACKET, who opposed some of the treaties, and favored a continuance of the war, by the Indians, on their own account.

In these and subsequent transactions, which the limits of this address prevent me from presenting in detail, CORNPLANTER exerted his power and influence in favor of peace. As early as 1791, he advocated the cultivation of the soil, and the adoption of the arts of civilized life, including the education of the Indian children. In a letter of that year to Friends in Philadelphia, he says: " Brothers, the Seneca nation see that the Great Spirit intends they should not continue to live by hunting, and they look around on every side and inquire, who it is that shall teach them what is best for them to do? Your fathers dealt honorably by our fathers, and they have engaged us to remember it. We wish our children to be taught the same principles by which your fathers were guided. Brothers! We have too little wisdom among us, and we cannot teach our children what we see their situation requires them to know. We wish them to be taught to read, and write, and such other things as you teach your children, especially the love of peace." I may here remark, that the Friends did respond to this call, and through a long series of years, put forth the most disinterested and philanthropic efforts in behalf of the Seneca nation.

In 1791, CORNPLANTER was employed by WASHINGTON, on behalf of the government of the United States, to proceed into the country of the North-Western Indians, then at war with the United States, on an embassy of peace and reconciliation. This arrangement was made during CORNPLANTER'S visit to Philadelphia in that year. Before proceeding on his mission, he returned to his home on the Allegheny, and soon afterwards called a Council of the Six Nations. The result of which was the appointment of representative Chiefs of the Six Nations, to attend a Council with the Western Indians. This Council was held at Au Glaize, (Fort Defiance, Ohio,) in October, 1792. CORNPLANTER, accompanied by a large number of the Chiefs of the League, was in attendance. The hostile Indians were determined to insist upon the river Ohio as their boundary; and besides the encroachments of the whites upon their territory, they had other grievances of which they complained. The Shawanese, especially, were opposed to peace, except upon such terms as they well knew would not be accepted by the United States. Their principal orator said: "The President well knows why the blood is so deep in our paths." CORNPLANTER'S efforts to effect a reconciliation between the Western tribes and the United States failed.*

CORNPLANTER, at this period, was perhaps the only Chief of the Senecas and Six Nations, who remained firm and unshaken in his friendship for the United States. About this time the repulse of General HARMAR, by the Western Indians, had greatly emboldened them, and it was with great difficulty that the peaceful suggestions of CORNPLANTER were acquiesced in by the Six Nations, many of whom still desired to make common cause with the Western tribes. In company with Colonel PROCTOR, of the United States army, he proceeded to the country of the hostile Indians, and endeavored to reconcile them to the United States. His mission failed,

* Western Annals, p. 606.

chiefly through the evil influences of BRANT and RED JACKET, aided by the machinations of British officers. At a subsequent period CORNPLANTER renewed his efforts for peace, and even called forth in favor of his measures, the opinions of the Indian women, who, as is natural to their sex, were the friends of peace. On this occasion, RED JACKET, among other remarks, said to the United States commissioners: "You know what we have been doing so long, and what trouble we have been at, and you know that it has been the request of our head warrior, CORNPLANTER, that we are left to answer for our women, who are to conclude what ought to be done." * * * *

"Colonel BUTLER, of the British, told us he must take our writings down to Colonel GORDON,* as he is a very wise man, and perhaps he may have something to say to us that may be for our good, and we want his assistance, as he is the man that keeps all the vessels that are on the Lake; therefore, my brother, make your mind easy, for your request is granted. And when we hear from our brothers, the British, then we shall know what time to start. And you must not be uneasy, that our brother, ABEEL, (CORNPLANTER,) can not go with you, for he is very tired, (referring to his former journey,) and must rest awhile, and take charge of our young warriors, to keep them in peace while they are playing— for fear of danger."

The intrigue of RED JACKET, aided by the action of the British officers, kept CORNPLANTER from this mission. There was, as suggested by a learned historian, Mr. STONE, (in his life of RED JACKET,) another reason

---

* The British commandant at Niagara.

lying still deeper in the minds of the Indian women, under whose influence these proceedings were had. CORNPLANTER was not only the principal war Chief of the Senecas, but he was a man of great bravery and sagacity, and withal a sincere friend of peace. The times were critical, and the Indians at Buffalo creek, and the adjacent country, were in frequent alarm. They wished to retain CORNPLANTER, as he could best restrain the warlike propensities of the young warriors, while they could repose greater confidence, both in his bravery and discretion, in the event of actual danger during the absence of the messengers to the Western Indians, than in any leader of their nation. This mission failed entirely. "The man that kept the vessels on the Lake," refused to recognize Colonel PROCTOR in his official capacity, and prohibited the passage of the Indian deputies to Sandusky, on Lake Erie, their place of destination.

A treaty held at Painted Post, in June, 1792, between Colonel PICKERING and the Six Nations, was productive of peaceful and good results. It checked the disposition of the young warriors to take part with the Western Indians, and it led to another mission of peace, at the head of which was the brave old Stockbridge Chief, HENRY AUPUMUT. It was also at this treaty, that WASHINGTON, through his agent, Colonel PICKERING, made an influential demonstration towards winning the attention of the Chiefs to the policy of having permanent habitations, where they could cultivate their lands, and commence the work of civilization among their people.

After this period, CORNPLANTER made another, but an unsuccessful embassy to the hostile Indians. His efforts being unavailing, the war with the Western Indians continued to rage until the year 1794, when, on the 20th of August of that year, Gen. WAYNE achieved his decisive victory over them at the battle of the Miami. It was mainly due to CORNPLANTER'S influence and exertions, that the Six Nations were not involved in that battle, and its fatal consequences to the hostile Indians engaged in it. Although the war with the Indians was terminated, there were perplexing questions to settle between the United States and the Six Nations, in which also, the States of Pennsylvania and New York were concerned. These were principally questions of boundaries, and also in reference to the grant of Presque Isle and the adjacent country. A Council was held at Buffalo creek, on the 18th of June, 1794, in reference to these difficulties. In this Council, CORNPLANTER took a conspicuous part; his speech on the occasion is fully reported in the proceedings. I make room for a single observation—addressing the commissioner as the representative of the President, he said: "Brother! You know our demands; we ask but for a small piece of land, and we trust, as you are a great man, you can easily grant our request." It is unnecessary, on this occasion, to give the details of this Council, nor of the Great Council which was soon after held at Canandaigua, namely, in October and November, 1794, at which CORNPLANTER, with other Chiefs, represented the Six Nations. Colonel PICKERING was again the commissioner on the part of the United States. The Friends of Pennsylvania and New Jersey, had also agents present, and exerted a highly beneficial influence.

Mr. STONE, to whose interesting work I am much indebted, speaking of this treaty, says: "This was the last general Council held by the United States with the Iroquois Confederacy, and a vast amount of important business was transacted thereat. Several perplexing questions of contested boundaries were settled, and the relations between the United States and the Confederacy were adjusted upon a basis that has not been since disturbed. CORNPLANTER arrived at this Council on the second day after the day assigned for the meeting. He came with four hundred of the Allegheny portion of the Senecas. There were sixteen hundred Indians collected on this interesting occasion. It appears that CORNPLANTER was subjected to some suspicions by his Indian associates, because of his frequent interviews with Colonel PICKERING. He was reminded by one of the Chiefs, that he was but a *War Chief*, and was exceeding the bounds of his proper department, by partaking too largely in the conduct of civil affairs. Colonel PICKERING interposed, and stated that the private interviews he had with CORNPLANTER were at his special request. This explanation was, for a time, satisfactory. Further evidences of the distinction between the War Chiefs and Sachems were exhibited on this occasion. RED JACKET speaks of CORNPLANTER and Captain BRANT, (the latter was not present,) as only War Chiefs, and the proceedings show that which does not appear in other transactions, namely: that there was a marked distinction between the *Chiefs* and the *Sachems*, the former having the direction of affairs belonging to war, and the latter having control of the civil government, under certain restrictions dependent upon popular opinion; and it appeared that they regarded the military power as entirely subordinate to the civil authorities. This single fact shows that the untutored Ho-de-no-sau-nee (United People,) had made no inconsiderable advance in the science of free government.

Subsequent transactions between the whites and the Indians, related to the sale of the lands of the latter. Their power as a nation was gone. Henceforth, if they were called together as a nation, or as separate tribes, it was only through the agency of individuals or companies, who desired to obtain grants of their lands. A treaty of this character was held at Big Tree, in 1797, (the site of the present town of Genessee New York,) in reference to a claim of ROBERT MORRIS, of Pennsylvania, the assignee of the State of Massachusetts, of an alleged pre-emption right to a portion of the territory of the Seneca tribe.

Without entering into the details of this treaty, or others of a similar character, I refer to it because it developed one of the principles of government of the Confederacy, heretofore but little known or noticed. An appeal was taken by the women, from the opinion and decision of the Sachems. CORNPLANTER being the principal War Chief, presented the appeal, whereupon the Council was re-opened, and the proceedings were recognized by the Sachems, FARMER'S BROTHER being their speaker, as being in accordance with their laws and customs. The re-consideration resulted in a change in the treaty beneficial to the Indians.

CORNPLANTER, at the head of his nation, as its principal War Chief, had resisted the encroachment of the whites to the extent of his abilities. But as we have shown, when the fortune of war, under the superior power of the Thirteen Fires, rendered further resistance impossible, he had, as a wise statesman, made the best terms of peace he could procure. After the Revolutionary war, he desired to maintain friendly relations with the United States; and to accomplish this object, he was ready, when urgent necessity required it, to part with considerable portions of the Indian territory. His course of conduct, in these transactions, was severely criticised by rival Chiefs, and under their influence, his popularity, with the main portion of his tribe, and with the other members of the Six Nations, was seriously reduced, if not entirely destroyed.

It was during the period of his decline in power and authority, that it is said he endeavored to regain his influence by inducing his half-brother, Ga-ne-o-di-yo, (otherwise called "Handsome Lake,") who was a Seneca Sachem, to assume the character of a prophet. It does not appear by any satisfactory evidence, that CORNPLANTER had any agency whatever in respect to the alleged revelations made by his singular and talented relative. In the account which Ga-ne-o-di-yo gives of the trance which led to his revelations, after stating that he had been ill for a long time, he says: "I resigned myself to the will of the Great Spirit, and nightly returned my thanks to Him, as my eyes were gladdened at evening, by the sight of the stars of Heaven. I viewed the ornamented Heavens at evening, through the opening in the roof of my lodge, with grateful feelings to my Creator. I had no assurance that the next evening I could contemplate His works; for this reason my acknowledgments to Him were more frequent and sincere. When night was gone, and the sun again shed his light upon the earth, I saw and acknowledged, in the return of day, His continued goodness to me and to all mankind. At length I began to have an inward conviction, that my end was near. I resolved once more to exchange friendly words with my people, and I sent my daughter to summon my brothers, Gy-ant-wa-chia, (CORNPLANTER,) and Ta-wan-nears, (BLACK-SNAKE,) to come to my cabin." The daughter hastened to deliver the message, but before she returned with Ta-wan-nears, (CORNPLANTER was not at hand,) the Sachem had fallen into a state of insensibility, and lay for many hours in that condition; after his recovery, he announced to his tribe what he regarded as a revelation of the Great Spirit to the Indians.*

As CORNPLANTER was the half-brother of the prophet, he was supposed to be in some way connected with these revelations, more especially, as the prophet strongly inculcated the principles of temperance, to which the Chief had been, for many years, a devoted advocate. RED JACKET, and others, used these transactions to the disadvantage of CORNPLANTER, and from thenceforth he ceased to take any part in the affairs of the Six Nations, and but little in that of the Seneca tribe generally, but devoted himself chiefly to his own clan of that tribe. This clan, or part of his tribe, had for many years been under his official and personal direction. Reference, before this period, is often made to the ABEEL Senecas, and in a map published in 1792, by READING

---

* MORGAN's League of the Iroquois. A most interesting work, dedicated to Colonel PARKER, a Seneca Indian, now an officer of the United States army, attached to the staff of General GRANT. Chapter 3d of this book is devoted to the pretended revelation of Ga-ne-o-di-yo, and the doctrines of the religion be inculcated.

HOWELL, a considerable portion of the country on the upper waters of the Conewango, and near Chatauque lake, is designated thus: "O'BEALS—Cayentona." *

In 1797, CORNPLANTER again visited Philadelphia, the seat of government of the United States. His principal object appears to have been to pay his respects to President WASHINGTON, and take an official leave of him on his retirement from the public service. His address to WASHINGTON, on this occasion, is marked with his usual good sense and eloquence. This address was fortunately preserved among the papers of THOMAS MORRIS, son of ROBERT MORRIS.†

General WASHINGTON'S answer was not preserved. As he entertained the highest respect and esteem for CORNPLANTER, no doubt his words to the Chief were expressive of his kind regards for his Indian friend, and his best wishes for the happiness and prosperity of the Seneca tribe.

From henceforth the career of CORNPLANTER was unconnected with the general history of his country. He fixed his permanent residence upon the tract of land on the Allegheny river, granted to him by the Commonwealth of Pennsylvania. The grant from the Commonwealth is dated March 16, 1796. In the patent the tract is designated "Planter's Field," and his town is called "Jennesadaga." It became his home in life, and is now his resting place in death. Here he directed his efforts to the civilization and moral improvement of his people, and as an efficient means to produce the result inculcated

---

* This map is in the possession of the Pennsylvania Historical Society; it was recently presented by SAMUEL AGNEW, Esq.

† See *infra*, page 90.

the principles of temperance—to which he had himself been long devoted.

In 1802 he visited President JEFFERSON, at the city of Washington, for counsel and encouragement. In Mr. JEFFERSON's excellent and characteristic letter to him, he expresses his approbation of CORNPLANTER's conduct, and adds: "Go on then, brother, in the great reformation you have undertaken. Persuade our Red Men to be sober, and to cultivate their lands; and their women to spin and weave for their families. * * * It will be a great glory to you to have been the instrument of so happy a change, and your children's children, from generation to generation, will repeat your name with love and gratitude forever. In all your enterprises for the good of your people, you may count with confidence on the aid and protection of the United States, and on the sincerity and zeal with which I am animated in the furthering of this humane work. You are our brethren of the same land; we wish you prosperity, as brethren should do." Thus encouraged, our Chief devoted his time and energies to the best interests of his people, and under his influence and example they made considerable advances in civilization and moral improvement.

When the war of 1812, with England, broke forth, CORNPLANTER, although then far advanced in years, yet he offered his services to the United States, to go on the war path, and accompanied by two hundred warriors of his nation, repaired to Franklin, Venango county, when he learned that Colonel SAMUEL DALE was about to march from that place to the frontiers with the Venango regiment. Arriving at Franklin, he called upon Colonel DALE, and desired a statement of the causes and objects of the war, which being satisfactorily explained to him, he made an address, in which he said: "That many years ago a boy came over the great waters and settled among his people of the Six Nations; sometime thereafter the father followed to keep him in subjection; the Indians helped the father, but the boy was too much for both, and drove the father home. And now, when the father had become an old man, and the boy a strong man, and a good neighbor to his nation, he wished to show his friendship for the Thirteen Fires by taking his two hundred warriors to assist to drive the old man across the great waters."— Colonel DALE was obliged to inform the Chief that he had no authority to receive his warriors into his regiment, or take them to the frontiers. CORNPLANTER insisted that his warriors ought not to stay at home and live idly in their wigwams whilst their white friends and brothers were upon the war path. So persistent was he in sending his warriors, that he could only be satisfied by the promise of Colonel DALE to send for them when their services were required, and when he should receive authority from the government to muster the Indians into the service of the United States, and that in the mean time he was to go home to his seat at Jennesadaga and have his warriors ready to respond at a moment's call. They were not called for by Colonel DALE, but CORNPLANTER sent a considerable number of his warriors to the American army; they acted as scouts, and were highly serviceable on the frontiers, and in the Niagara campaign. His son, HENRY ABEEL, led these warriors; he held the the commission of major, and did good service to the United States in that war.

The condition of CORNPLANTER's town in 1816, is thus

described by Rev. TIMOTHY ALDEN, of Allegheny college, Meadville, Pa., who visited it in that year: "Jennesadaga, CORNPLANTER'S village, is on a handsome piece of bottom land, and comprises about a dozen buildings. It was grateful to notice the agricultural habits of the place, and the numerous enclosures of buckwheat, corn and oats. We also saw a number of oxen, cows and horses, and many logs designed for the saw-mill and the Pittsburg market. Last year, (1815,) the Western Missionary society established a school in the village, under Mr. SAMUEL OLDHAM. CORNPLANTER, as soon as apprised of our arrival, came over to see us and took charge of our horses. Though having many around him to obey his commands, yet in the ancient patriarchal style, he choose to serve us himself, and actually went into the field, cut the oats and fed our beasts. He appears to be about sixty-eight years of age,[*] and five feet ten inches in height. His countenance is strongly marked with intelligence and reflection. Contrary to the aboriginal custom, his chin is covered with a beard three or four inches in length. His house is of princely dimensions compared with most Indian huts, and has a piazza in front. He is owner of thirteen hundred acres of excellent land, six hundred of which encircle the ground-plot of his little town. He receives an annual stipend from the United States, of two hundred and fifty dollars. CORNPLANTER'S brother, lately deceased, (called the Prophet,) was known by the high-sounding name, Goskukewanna Kannedia, or Large Beautiful Lake."

Thus, in the altitude and with the authority of an an-

---

[*] Mr. ALDEN was deceived by appearances. CORNPLANTER was at that time, about eighty-four years of age.

cient patriarch, he continued to preside over his people, and promote their prosperity and improvement, without interruption or molestation, until the year 1822, when the authorities of Warren county, within the bounds of which he resided, attempted to levy taxes upon him and his clan. The old Chief had never before been called on for that purpose, and he objected to their payment. An armed sheriff's *posse* was called out to enforce the payment, but arriving near CORNPLANTER'S town, it was deemed prudent to send forward a few of their number to confer with the Chief. When they came to his house, they noticed a considerable number of Indians lounging about, and some of them were partly concealed in the bushes near by. CORNPLANTER received the committee with great dignity. The interview took place near his house, and around the sides of it were arranged about one hundred rifles. When asked for the payment of the taxes, the old warrior sternly refused, and pointing to the guns, said, "an Indian for each rifle;" and in response to his call, his clansmen sprang forward to the house. Whereupon the sheriff and his men withdrew, without enforcing the claim. CORNPLANTER afterwards, for the sake of peace, went to Warren, and gave his note for the amount of the taxes. This note was never collected. The Legislature of Pennsylvania released the taxes, and exonerated him and his heirs forever, from the payment of taxes on the lands granted to him by the Commonwealth.* The Governor sent commissioners to explain the transaction. CORNPLANTER met the commissioners at the court house in Warren, when he made a characteristic and appropriate address.†

---

* Journal House of Representatives, 1822-3.
† This address is fully presented in DAY's Historical Collections, p. 656.

This tax collector's raid would afford a fine subject for a painter: the romantic scenery of the Allegheny river, the old warrior's wigwam, the rifles arranged around it, the Indians in the bush, the last war-whoop of the old Chief as he called his men to the rescue—worthy of perpetuation as the expiring flash of the war-like fire of the last War Chief of his tribe.

THOMAS STRUTHERS, Esq., of Warren, was well acquainted with CORNPLANTER; at my request, he has furnished the following statement of an interview he had with the Chief in 1831: " In 1831, I accompanied some gentlemen, residents of Pittsburg and Butler, who desired to pay their respects to him. It was a pleasant day in May, when we called on him. He talked no English. I introduced the gentlemen through an interpreter, whom I had engaged, and informed him that they had called to pay their respects to him. He seemed much pleased that his white friends were inclined to pay him such attention. The introduction took place in front of his log cabin, on the bank of the Allegheny river. He gave orders to some young Indians, the import of which we soon ascertained, by the fact that they immediately collected some boards, and placed them for seats around a log sled, in the form of a hollow square. This done, the old Chief pointed out to each of the party his seat, and all sat facing inward. He then took his seat in the centre, and announced that he was prepared to hear any communications we had to make. I told him we had not come to buy lands or timber, nor to trade for furs and skins, but had called on him in the spirit of friendship, to pay our respects to the great Indian Chief, whom we had learned to admire as a warrior, and especially as the friend of the United States, who had inculcated the principles of peace and christianity among his people. I referred briefly to the schools established among his people by the Friends of Philadelphia.

"The old Chief replied in a speech, which would compare well with many of our best State papers. His manner was dignified and eloquent, and his eye lit up, as if by inspiration; so that it was very interesting to listen to what he said, although we could not understand it, until the interpreter rendered it to us. He spoke of the relations between the white men and the red men—the war and bloodshed caused by the former, to displace the latter from their hunting grounds—the peace effected with the Six Nations—dwelt particularly on the virtues of General WASHINGTON, the great and good White Father. He brought forth from a well covered valise, in which they were carefully wrapped in linen cloth, two or three "talks," as he termed them, on parchment, to which was appended the autograph of WASHINGTON. He said he had met WASHINGTON a number of times, and treated with him. His *single eye* sparkled with animation, when his name was mentioned. And in conclusion, he thanked the Great Spirit that there were now no wars or blood-shedding going on, but that peace and good will existed amongst all men and all nations, so far as he could hear. He spoke as a statesman and philanthropist, whose mind was occupied with the weighty interests of mankind, rather than with merely the affairs and concerns of a family or tribe. He thanked us for our call upon him, and invited us to dine with him, which we accepted. The bill of fare was jerked venison and corn mush; the latter was prepared in the Indian manner; each guest having a tin pan about half-full of hot water, in which the Indian meal was mixed at the pleasure of the guest."

The personal appearance of CORNPLANTER, towards the close of his long and eventful life, is well described by Judge THOMPSON, now of the Supreme Court of Pennsylvania, in an article written in 1836, and re-produced in DAY's Historical Collections of Pennsylvania, p. 657. I had a professional interview with the aged Chief, in the summer of 1835, to which I have already briefly referred. His personal appearance was therefore known to me. I agree with Judge THOMPSON, in his description of him, and as the article contains other interesting remarks, I insert it here, as follows:

"I once saw the aged and venerable Chief, and had an interesting interview with him about a year and a half before his death. I thought of many things, when seated near him beneath the wide spreading shade of an old sycamore, on the banks of the Allegheny; many things to ask him; the scenes of the revolution; the generals that fought its battles and conquered the Indians; his tribe; the Six Nations, and himself. He was constitutionally sedate; was never observed to smile, much less to indulge in the luxury of a laugh. When I saw him he estimated his age to be over one hundred years. I think one hundred and three was about his reckoning of it. This would make him near one hundred and five years old at the time of his decease. His person was much stooped, and his stature was far short of what it once had been—not being over five feet six inches at the time I speak of. Mr. JOHN STRUTHERS, of Ohio, told me, some years since, that he had seen him near fifty years ago, and at that period he was about his height, viz: six feet, one inch. Time and hardship had made dreadful impressions upon that ancient form. The chest was sunken and his shoulders were drawn forward, making the upper part of his body resemble a trough. His limbs had lost their symmetry, and become crooked. His feet, too, (for he had taken off his moccasins,) were deformed and haggard by injury. I would say that most of his fingers on one hand were useless; the sinews had been severed by a blow of the tomahawk or scalping knife. How I longed to ask him what scene of blood and strife had thus stamped the enduring evidence of its existence upon his person. But to have done so, would, in all probability, have put an end to all further conversation on any subject. The information desired, would certainly not have been received, and I had to forego my curiosity. He had but one eye, and even the socket of the lost organ was hid by the overhanging brow resting upon the high cheek bone. His remaining eye was of the brightest and blackest hue. Never have I seen one, in young or old, that equalled it in brilliancy. Perhaps it had borrowed lustre from the eternal darkness that rested on its neighboring orbit. His ears had been dressed in the Indian mode, all but the outside had been cut away; on the one ear the ring had been torn asunder near the top, and hung down his neck like a useless rag. He had a full head of hair, white as the driven snow, which covered a head of ample dimensions and admirable shape. His face was not swarthy, but this may be accounted for from the fact, that he was but half Indian. He told me that he had been at Franklin, more than eighty years before the period of our conversation, on his passage down the Ohio and Mississippi, with the warriors of his tribe, on some expedition against the Creeks or Osages. He had long been a man of peace, and I believe his great characteristics were humanity and truth.

"It is said that BRANT and THE CORNPLANTER were never friends after the massacre of Cherry valley. Some have alleged, because the Wyoming massacre was, in part, perpetrated by the Senecas, that THE CORNPLANTER was there. Of the justice of this suspicion, there are many reasons for doubt. It is certain that he was not the Chief of the Senecas at that time.

"As he stood before me—the ancient Chief in ruins— how forcibly was I struck with the truth of the beautiful figure of the old aboriginal Chieftain, who, in describing himself, said 'he was like an aged hemlock, dead at the top, and whose branches alone were green.' After more than one hundred years of most varied life—of strife—of danger—of peace—he at last slumbers in deep repose on the banks of his own beloved Allegheny."

Pennsylvania has acted with liberality and kindness to this venerated Chief. She granted to him three valuable tracts of land; on one of which he had fixed his residence. It is the place where he now rests in the quietude of the grave.

The first report on the subject of these grants to CORNPLANTER, is dated March 24, 1789. It is contained in a communication from General MIFFLIN, then President of the Supreme Executive Council of Pennsylvania, to RICHARD PETERS, Speaker of the General Assembly, in which he encloses General RICHARD BUTLER's letter, recommending the grant of fifteen hundred acres of land to THE CORNPLANTER, a Seneca Chief.* General BUT-LER's letter is dated March 23, 1789. In it he says: "I beg leave to mention, that Captain ABEEL, *alias* THE CORNPLANTER, one of the principal Chiefs of the Seneca tribe of the Six Nations, has been very useful in all the treaties since 1784, inclusive, and particularly to the State of Pennsylvania; this he has demonstrated very fully, and his attachment, at present, to the State, appears very great. This has induced me to suggest to your Excellency and Council, whether it may not be good policy to fix this attachment by making it his interest to continue it. This, from the ideas he possesses of civilization, induces me to think if the State would be pleased to grant him a small tract of land within the late purchase, it would be very grateful to him, and have that effect. This may be done in a manner that would render him service without lessening his influence with his own people. The quantity need not be large; perhaps one thousand or fifteen hundred acres. My wishes for the quiet and interest of the State, as well as the merits of the man, induced me to mention this matter."†

The Great Founder of Pennsylvania established his government on "deeds of peace." He has the unquestioned pre-eminence of having treated the aboriginal inhabitants with greater justice and rectitude than any other Proprietor or Founder of an American State.— "The settlement of this Province (Pennsylvania) was founded on the principles of truth, equity and mercy, and the blessings of divine Providence attended the early care of the first founders to impress these principles on

---

* Colonial Records of Pennsylvania, volume I, p. 37.
† Pennsylvania Archives, 1786-90, p. 562.

the minds of the native inhabitants; so that when their numbers were great, and their strength vastly superior, they received our ancestors with gladness, relieved their wants with open hearts, granted them peaceable possession of the land, and for a long course of time gave constant and frequent proofs of a cordial friendship."* It is, therefore, an appropriate testimonial to the character of Penn, as well as to that of Cornplanter, that the Commonwealth of Pennsylvania should, by her constituted authorities, cause the erection of this monument to the memory of this worthy and distinguished Indian Chief. And it is the only monument, so far as my knowledge extends, erected by public authority in the United States, either national, or sub-national, to the memory of an Indian Chief.

The character of the venerable Cornplanter has been exhibited, though I fear imperfectly, in this sketch of his life and services. We have seen that he was a brave warrior and chieftain, an able statesman and an eloquent orator. In the latter part of his life, especially, his prominent characteristics were a love of peace and temperance. And it is believed by those who knew him best, that the truths of christianity had made a deep impression on his mind. A circumstance which occurred about the year 1822, has been cited by several writers as an evidence of his return to the superstitions of his race. I refer to his destroying a sword and pistols, and some other military accoutrements which had been presented to him by Washington, and a gold laced hat which was given him by Governor Mifflin; also a French flag and superb belt

---

* Address to Governor Morris by the "people called Quakers," April 12, 1756. Manuscript Historical Society of Pennsylvania.

of wampum, trophies of valor, which had been for several generations in his family, in honor of some of his mother's ancestors, who won them in battle from the French. It is alleged that he did this act in a moment of alarm, as if the Great Spirit had moved him to destroy the memorials of his friendly relations with the whites. On the contrary, it clearly appears that under the influence of christianity, particularly as evinced in the teachings of the Society of Friends, who had established schools in his nation, he became so firm an advocate of peace, that he wished to remove from him all the memorials that re-called to his recollection the scenes of war and blood through which he had passed. He carefully preserved the memorials of peace of which he was in possession. I myself noticed, for he exhibited them to me, how great a regard he had for the parchment documents which he possessed, that were subscribed by WASHINGTON; and with what scrupulous care and painstaking he had preserved them. These papers, and others of a like character, are now in the possession of the family of CORNPLANTER, and are most interesting historical memorials. Their preservation, in such manner as may be agreeable to the descendants of the Chief, is a matter of interest and solicitude to all persons who properly appreciate such materials of history.

Those who knew CORNPLANTER personally, had the greatest respect for him. Dr. IRVINE, of Brokenstraw, a son of General C. IRVINE, an intimate friend of the Chief, in a letter to me, says: "I frequently heard my father say, that CORNPLANTER was one of the most honest and truthful men he ever knew, whether white or red." Judge JOHNSON, of Warren, under whose direction this (CORNPLANTER) monument is erected, states to me, "so far as he was personally known to residents in this section of country, he was regarded as a living example of integrity, truthfulness, purity, temperance, fatherly affection for his tribe and race, and a generous Indian hospitality to all. He possessed the universal affection and veneration of his tribe and of all men who knew him."

Such was the life and career of CORNPLANTER; and such his character as shown from history, from the testimony of contemporaries, and of living witnesses. He died in this Indian village, (Jennesadaga,) on the 18th of February, 1836, aged about one hundred and five years.

This is no ordinary occasion. A great Commonwealth, by a solemn act of legislation, and by her agents here this day, honors the memory of the distinguished Indian Chief, whose mortal remains lie mouldering in this grave. We this day dedicate this monument to the memory of CORNPLANTER, an Indian Chief of the Seneca tribe and of the Six Nations—and may we, both white men and red men, and our children's children, as long as this beautiful river bears its waters to the ocean, venerate his memory and emulate his virtues.

ADDENDUM.

I have recently examined Mr. KETCHUM's history of Buffalo and the Senecas. The *facts* he presents corroborate the views I have presented of the character and services of CORNPLANTER. I am surprised, however, to notice that he expresses an *opinion* adverse to our Chief. He does him great injustice when he says: "There is no doubt that CORNPLANTER was at heart in the British interest, up to the period of WAYNE's victory in 1794." He also makes the extraordinary assertion, that CORNPLANTER acted in concert with BRANT, during the period of the Indian troubles in Ohio, after the Revolutionary war!

The contrary most clearly appears by the whole course of conduct of our Chief; as well as by his speeches, his letters and his participation in treaties. With BRANT, CORNPLANTER never was on friendly terms, and after the war of the Revolution, their policy, and even personal relations, were adverse and hostile. Mr. KETCHUM, himself, shows that there existed between these Chiefs "a personal dislike."

While CORNPLANTER was aiding WASHINGTON and his agents, Colonels PROCTOR and PICKERING, and others, to preserve peace with the hostile Indians of the west, and conciliate the Six Nations, BRANT was the agent of the British to keep up the war, and he even sent some of his warriors to join the enemy, when they took up the hatchet; he made his home with the British, and was in constant communication with Colonels GORDON and M'KEE, the commanders at Niagara and Detroit, and with other British officers.

The writer referred to adds the following: "As a warrior, whatever may be thought or said by whites, CORNPLANTER, in the estimation of the Indians who were their cotemporaries, was the superior of BRANT. The Senecas were a nation of warriors; and it will be admitted that they did the most of the fighting for the Six Nations, during nearly two centuries of their history, with which we are conversant. From the time CORNPLANTER came on the stage, (and he entered upon the war path early,) down to the close of the Revolutionary war, he had no superior, and few equals as a warrior. His other qualifications will be judged by the record he has left in his speeches and letters, and in the archives of our State and National Government."—Vol. 1, p. 411.

I am content to let the personal and political character of our Chief be judged by the records thus referred to. And I think I have shown in this MEMORIAL, *from these records*, that CORNPLANTER was not only a distinguished warrior, statesman and orator, but that he was, after the close of the Revolutionary war, the active, faithful and devoted friend of the government and people of the United States. And that he also well deserves the inscription on the monument erected by Pennsylvania to his memory, "Distinguished for talent, courage, eloquence, sobriety and love for his tribe and race, to whose welfare he devoted his time, his energies and his means, during a long and eventful life."

There is one trait in the character of CORNPLANTER, not heretofore noticed, which is referred to by Colonel PROCTOR in his narrative, and which I think ought to be presented here. Colonel PROCTOR was sent by WASHINGTON, to visit CORNPLANTER, to engage him and other

Chiefs, to go on an embassy of peace to the Western Indians. He traveled by way of Wyoming and the Susquehanna. I quote from his narrative, under the date of March 20, 1791.

"This day we set forward for Captain Waterman Baldwin's, above Wilkesbarre; arrived there in the evening, halted for him part of two days, as I had orders to take him with me to the residence of THE CORNPLANTER, at which place he was intended to act as instructor to the Indian youth, as also a director in the mode and management of agriculture, for the use and benefit of the Indians. This gentleman was made prisoner by CORNPLANTER during the late war, (Revolution,) *and was treated by him with remarkable tenderness, until legally exchanged.*"

ADDRESSES
OF
JOHN LUKE AND STEPHEN S. SMITH.

The following addresses were then made by the Indians herein mentioned; they were translated by HARRISON HALFTOWN and BENJAMIN WILLIAMS, both Senecas. Mr. SNOWDEN took notes of these addresses, and has written them out as follows:

JOHN LUKE, a councillor of the Seneca nation, said: Brothers! White men and Indians:—It has been laid upon me to say a few words. We were well pleased when we heard that the State of Pennsylvania had directed that a monument should be put up to the memory of CORNPLANTER, at his grave. And we were pleased when word came to us that the white people and Indians should be here to-day to see the monument set in its proper place, and to hear what our white brothers should say on the occasion. We are thankful for what has been done by Pennsylvania, and for the good words we have heard this beautiful day. The occasion will long be remembered by us. This monument, more enduring than the wampum which our forefathers used to record events and keep them in remembrance, will remind us of the kindness of Pennsylvania to our great and good Chief, and keep bright the chain whose links have united us to the Quaker State even from the time of ONAS (WILLIAM PENN) to the present day. Brothers! THE CORNPLANTER was known to us to be an honest man, and without deceit, and we are glad to hear, by the words spoken this day, that our white brethren so regard him, and respect his memory. He made the treaties and speeches referred to this day, and I now say that it is proper that all the people should remember that every word that has been said, so far as I understand them, are words of truth. We always understood that CORNPLANTER desired his children, and his nation, to follow the example of the white people in cultivating the land. It lies upon our hearts that we should remember the words of THE CORNPLANTER.

Friendship was established between the red men and the white men by treaties, and we wish them to stand permanent. This is all I have to say in behalf of my people. Farewell!

STEPHEN S. SMITH, a Seneca Indian, and a Chief of the Six Nations, then rose and said: Friends and Brothers! We are grateful for what is done and said here this beautiful day. The sun shines upon us, and we are here as brothers to do honor to the memory of old CORNPLANTER. It is in accordance with the laws and customs of the Six Nations that the people should meet to commemorate the memory of the dead.

Brothers! We are now a feeble people in numbers and in power; our forefathers were strong and powerful. This is known to us, and it is grateful to our hearts to hear the history of the Six Nations described to us to-day. It is gratifying to us to hear the words we have heard this day, so true and plain, delivered by our brother, from Philadelphia, who so well depicted the life and character of CORNPLANTER. And here at his grave, where his bones are buried, it is our duty to remember his in structions to his people, to work, and also, to plant our land; and now it is our duty to prosecute that work as his children. Brothers! We have been told that the Indians are like the leaves which fall at this season of the year. The leaves do fall, but we live in hope that the next summer will bring them forth again. My wish is, that what remains of the Six Nations, and their children's children, should continue to live on the lands which they now own by means of reservations secured to them by the States of New York and Pennsylvania. I am not willing to see the day when these hills will no longer look down upon the cabins of our people. I hope they will live here, and on the New York reservations, neighbors of our friends, the white people, until we and they are called away unto the place of everlasting rest; where there is but one people, one mind and one tongue. I hope our children, to the remotest generations, will come here and look at this monument to old CORNPLANTER, and read what is inscribed upon it; and my desire is that the Indians of the Seneca nation should continue to live here, not only as long as this handsome monument stands, but as long as these hills and valleys remain, and the waters of the Allegheny mingle with the Ohio and Mississippi. And now, on behalf of my nation, I return thanks to the State of Pennsylvania, and to our white brethren present, for what has been so well done this day; and say to all farewell.

NOTE BY J. R. SNOWDEN.

The following is a brief statement of the present location and population of the Six Nations of Indians:

SENECAS.

1. Senecas on the Allegheny river, in Pennsylvania, fifteen miles above Warren, at CORNPLANTER'S town, (Jennesadaga.)
Population 80
Acres of land owned 300

2. Senecas on the Allegheny reservation, in New York, a few miles above the Pennsylvania line.
Population about 900
Acres of land 26,600

3. Senecas on Cattaraugus reservation, in Erie and Cattaraugus counties, New York.
Population about 1,700
Acres of land under cultivation 5,000

4. Senecas at Tonawandas, in New York.
Population about 700
Acres of land 7,000

ONEIDAS.

1. Oneidas, in Oneida and Madison counties N. York.
Population about 250
Acres of land 400

2. The largest remnant of this tribe, (Oneidas,) reside in Brown county, Wisconsin.
Population about 800
They possess a large body of land.

ONONDAGOS.

The residence of this tribe is about six miles south of the city of Syracuse, in the State of New York.

Population about............................. 350
Acres of land owned........................ 7,600

TUSCARORAS.

Their residence is about seven miles north-east of Niagara Falls.

Population about............................. 350
Acres of land held by them.................. 6,250

RECAPITULATION OF POPULATION.

Senecas.. 3,380
Oneidas.. 1,050
Onondagos..................................... 350
Tuscaroras..................................... 350

Total....................................... 5,130

The present condition of these remnants of the Six Nations is quite respectable. In most of the reservations they have schools and places of public worship. Many of them belong to the Methodist and Baptist churches. The Chief of the Six Nations, STEPHEN S. SMITH, who made a speech at the inauguration of the CORNPLANTER monument, is a minister in the Baptist church. He is a man of intelligence and respectability. I here insert a letter I have recently received from him, which will doubtless be interesting to our readers.

"AKRON, N. Y., *July* 10, 1867.

"DEAR SIR:—I am very desirous of obtaining a copy of the history of the life of CORNPLANTER. If you have a copy of the history that you spoke at the raising of the monument on the CORNPLANTER reservation last October, and will send it to me for the use and benefit of our young men, you will confer a favor upon me and them that I shall be most grateful to re-pay, when an opportunity is presented. And if you have a copy of the minutes of the addresses delivered that day, and taken by yourself, I should be most happy to receive a copy of the same also.

"If your noble State saw fit to appropriate money to fence the grave of the deceased CORNPLANTER, I shall be most happy to meet you there and assist you in surrounding the last resting place of our departed brother, with the respectful barricade furnished by a grateful people.

"I am sorry, that it is necessary, in speaking of our honored brother, JOHN LUKE, who was with us at the monument meeting last October, that he will be with us no more at our meetings this side of the setting sun. He took his departure for the great spiritual hunting ground last April.

"Yours truly,
"STEPHEN S. SMITH,
"*Chief of Six Nations.*

"To JAMES ROSS SNOWDEN, Philadelphia."

An appropriation having been made for that object, by the Legislature at its last session, a substantial and appropriate fence was placed around the grave and monument of CORNPLANTER on the 20th of September, 1867. It consists of marble posts with carved caps; iron rails with chains and tassels, and presents a very handsome appearance.

In honor of the completion of the monument, and to express their thanks to the Great Spirit, and their gratitude to the Commonwealth of Pennsylvania and her agents, the Senecas had a "green corn feast," on the 23d, 24th and 25th of September. It was a great occasion, and was largely attended. Their ceremonies had relation not only to the completion of the monument, but to express their thanks to the Great Spirit for the abundant crops which have this year rewarded their agricultural labors. The erection of the CORNPLANTER monument, and the proceedings relating to it, have had an excellent and benign influence upon these Indians. A friend writes to me: "The natives are greatly pleased with all that has been done; they have better crops than usual, and act more civilized. These proceedings have increased their self-respect, and made an enduring mark upon their grateful hearts."

APPENDIX.

JOINT RESOLUTION AUTHORIZING THE CORNPLANTER MONUMENT.

The Joint Resolution of the Legislature of Pennsylvania, authorizing the erection of the monument to CORNPLANTER, is in the following words:

WHEREAS, SOLOMON O'BAIL, a grandson of CORNPLANTER, an Indian, who rendered eminent services to the State and Nation, during the Revolutionary war and the early history of Pennsylvania, and MARK PIERCE, his interpreter, have just had a hearing before the Senate:

AND WHEREAS, A recognition of the eminent services of CORNPLANTER, is due from the government of Pennsylvania; therefore,

Be it Resolved by the Senate and House of Representatives of the Commonwealth of Pennsylvania in General Assembly met, That the State Treasurer shall pay to SOLOMON O'BAIL, the sum of five hundred dollars out of any moneys in the treasury not otherwise appropriated, and the further sum of five hundred dollars to SAMUEL P. JOHNSON, to be expended in erecting and enclosing a suitable monument in memory of CORNPLANTER.

(Signed) JAMES R. KELLEY,
Speaker of the House of Representatives.

DAVID FLEMING,
Speaker of the Senate.

APPROVED—The twenty-fifth day of January, Anno Domini one thousand eight hundred and sixty-six.

A. G. CURTIN.

SPEECH OF CORNPLANTER,

TO PRESIDENT WASHINGTON, AT PHILADELPHIA, IN THE YEAR 1790.

FATHER! The voice of the Seneca nation speaks to you, the great councillor, in whose heart the wise men of all the Thirteen Fires have placed their wisdom. It may be very small in your ears, and we therefore entreat you to hearken with attention, for we are about to speak of things which are to us very great. When your army entered the country of the Six Nations, we called you the Town Destroyer; and to this day, when that name is heard, our women look behind them and turn pale, and our children cling to the necks of their mothers. Our councillors and warriors are men, and cannot be afraid; but their hearts are grieved with the fears of our women and children, and desire it may be buried so deep as to be heard no more. When you gave us peace, we called you father, because you promised to secure us in the possession of our lands. Do this, and so long as the lands shall remain, that beloved name shall live in the heart of every Seneca.

Father! We mean to open our hearts before you, and we earnestly desire that you will let us clearly understand what you resolve to do. When our Chiefs returned from the treaty at Fort Stanwix, and laid before our council what had been done there, our nation was surprised to hear how great a country you had compelled them to give up to you without your paying, to us, anything for it. Every one said that your hearts were yet swelled with resentment against us for what had happened during the war, but that one day you would re-consider it with more kindness. We asked each other, "What have we done to deserve such severe chastisement?"

Father! When you kindled your Thirteen Fires separately, the wise men assembled at them told us that you were all brothers, the children of one great father, who regarded, also, the red people as his children. They called us brothers, and invited us to his protection; they told us that he resided beyond the great water where the sun first rises; that he was a King, whose power no people could resist, and that his goodness was as bright as that sun. What they said went to our hearts, we accepted the invitation, and promised to obey him. What the Seneca nation promise they faithfully perform, and when you refused obedience to that King, he commanded us to assist his beloved men in making you sober. In obeying him, we did no more than yourselves had led us to promise. The men that claimed this promise told us you were children and had no guns; that when they had shaken you, you would submit. We hearkened to them, and were deceived, until your army approached our towns. We were deceived; but your people, in teaching us to confide in that King, helped to deceive us, and we now appeal to your heart—is the blame all ours?

Father! When we saw that we were deceived, and heard the invitation which you gave us to draw near to the fire which you had kindled, and talk with you concerning peace, we made haste towards it. You then told us that we were in your hand, and that by closing it you could crush us to nothing, and you demanded from us a great country as the price of that peace which you had offered us—as if our want of strength had destroyed our rights. Our Chiefs had felt your power, and were unable to contend against you, and they, therefore, gave up that country. What they agreed to has bound our nation, but your anger against us must by this time be cooled, and although our strength has not increased, nor your power become less, we ask you to consider calmly, were the terms dictated to us by your commissioners reasonable and just?

Father! Your commissioners, when they drew the line which separated the land then given up to you, from that which you agreed should remain to be ours, did most solemnly promise that we should be secured in the peaceable possession of the lands which we inhabited east and north of that line. Does this promise bind you?

Hear now, we beseech you, what has happened concerning that land. On the day in which we finished the treaty at Fort Stanwix, commissioners from Pennsylvania told our Chiefs that they had come there to purchase all the lands belonging to us within the lines of their State, and they told us that their line would strike the river Susquehanna, below Tioga Branch. They then left us to consider of the bargain till next day. On the next day, we let them know that we were unwilling to sell all the lands within their State, and proposed to let them have part of it, which we pointed out to them in their map. They told us that they must have the whole; that it was already ceded to them by the great King, at the time of making peace with you, and was *their own;* but they said that they would not take advantage of that, and were willing to pay us for it—after the manner of their ancestors. Our Chiefs were unable to contend at that time, and, therefore, they sold the lands up to the line which was then shown to them as the line of that State. What the commissioners had said about the land having been ceded to them at the peace, our Chiefs considered as intended only to lessen the price, and they passed it by with very little notice; but since that we have heard so much from others, about the right to our lands, which the King gave when you made peace with him, that it is our earnest desire that you will tell us what it means.

Father! Our nation empowered JOHN LIVINGSTON to let out part of our lands on rent, to be paid to us. He told us that he was sent by Congress to do this for us, and we fear he has deceived us in the writing he has obtained from us. For since the time of our giving that power, a man of the name of PHELPS has come among us, and claimed our whole country, northward of the line of Pennsylvania, under purchase from that LIVINGSTON, to whom he said he had paid twenty thousand dollars for it. He said, also, that he had bought, likewise, from the Council of the Thirteen Fires, and paid them twenty thousand dollars more for the same. And he said, also, that it did not belong to us, for the great King had ceded the whole of it when you made peace with him. Thus he claimed the whole country north of Pennsylvania, and west of the lands belonging to the Cayugas. He demanded it; he insisted on his demand, and declared that he would have it *all*. It was impossible for us to grant him this, and we immediately refused it. After some days, he proposed to run a line at a small distance eastward of our western boundary, which we refused to agree to. He then threatened us with immediate war if we did not comply.

Upon this threat, our Chiefs held a council, and they agreed that no event of war could be worse than to be driven, with our wives and children, from the only country which we had any right to, and, therefore, weak as our nation was, they determined to take the chance of war, rather than submit to such unjust demands, which seemed to have no bounds. STREET, the great trader to Niagara, was then with us, having come at the request of PHELPS, and as he always professed to be our great friend, we consulted him upon this subject. He also told us that our lands had been ceded by the King, and that we *must* give them up.

Astonished at what we heard from every quarter, with hearts aching with compassion for our women and children, we were thus compelled to give up all our country north of the line of Pennsylvania, and east of the Genesee river, up to the fork, and east of a south line drawn from that fork to the Pennsylvania line.

For this land, PHELPS agreed to pay us ten thousand dollars in hand, and one thousand forever. He paid us two thousand dollars, and five hundred dollars in hand, part of the ten thousand, and he sent for us to come last spring and receive our money, but instead of paying us the remainder of the ten thousand, and the one thousand dollars due for the first year, he offered us no more than five hundred dollars, and insisted that he agreed with us for that sum, to be paid yearly. We debated with him for six days, during which time he persisted in refusing to pay us our just demand, and he insisted that we should receive the five hundred dollars; and STREET, from Niagara, also insisted on our receiving the money as it was offered to us. The last reason he assigned for continuing to refuse paying was, *that the King had ceded all the lands to the Thirteen Fires*, and that he had bought them from you, and *paid you for them*.

We could bear this confusion no longer; and determined to press through every difficulty, and lift up our voice that you might hear us, and to claim that security in the possession of our lands, which your commissioners promised us. And we now entreat you to inquire into our complaints, and redress our wrongs.

Father! Our writings were lodged in the hands of STREET, of Niagara, as we supposed him to be our friend; but when we saw PHELPS consulting with STREET, on every occasion, we doubted of his honesty towards us, and we have since heard that he was to receive, for his endeavors to deceive us, a piece of land ten miles in width, west of the Genesee river, and near forty miles in length, extending to Lake Ontario; and the lines of this tract have been run accordingly, although no part of it is within the bounds which limits his purchase. No doubt he meant to deceive us.

Father! You have said that we are in your hand, and that by closing it you could crush us to nothing. Are you determined to crush us? If you are, tell us so; that those of our nation who have become your children, and have determined to die so, may know what to do.

In this case, one Chief has said he would ask you to put him out of pain. Another, who will not think of dying by the hand of his father or his brother, has said he will retire to the Chatanque, eat of the fatal root, and sleep with his fathers in peace.

Before you determine on a measure so unjust, look up to God, who has made *us* as well as *you*. We hope he will not permit you to destroy the whole of our nations.

Father! Hear our case; many nations inhabited this country, but they had no wisdom, and therefore they warred together. The Six Nations were powerful, and compelled them to peace; the lands, for a great extent, were given up to them, but the nations which were not destroyed, all continued on those lands, and claimed the protection of the Six Nations, as the brothers of their fathers. They were men, and when at peace, had a right to live on the earth. The French came among us and built Niagara; they became our fathers, and took care of us. Sir WILLIAM JOHNSON came and took that Fort from the French; he became our father, and promised to take care of us, and did so, until you were too strong for his King. To him we gave four miles around Niagara, as a place of trade. We have already said how we came to join against you; we saw that we were wrong; we wished for peace; you demanded a great country to be given up to you; it was surrendered to you, as the price of peace, and we ought to have peace, and possession of the little land which you then left us.

Father! When that great country was given up, there were but few Chiefs present, and they were compelled to give it up, and it is not the Six Nations, only, that reproach these Chiefs with having given up that county, the Chippewas, and all the nations who lived on those lands westward, call to us, and ask us "Brothers of our fathers, where is the place you have reserved for us to lie down upon?"

Father! You have compelled us to do that which has made us ashamed. We have nothing to answer to the children of the brothers of our fathers. When, last spring, they called upon us to go to war to secure them a bed to lie upon, the Senecas entreated them to be quiet, till we had spoken to you

But on our way down, we heard that your army had gone toward the country which those nations inhabit, and if they meet together, the best blood on both sides will stain the ground.

Father! We will not conceal from you that the Great God and not man has preserved THE CORNPLANTER from the hands of his own nation. For they ask continually "where is the land which our children, and their children after them, are to lie down upon." You to us say, that the line drawn from Pennsylvania to Lake Ontario would mark it forever on the east, and the line running from Buffalo creek to Pennsylvania would mark it on the west, and we see that it is not so. For first one, and then another, comes and takes it away by order of that people which you tell us promises to secure it to us. He is silent, for he has nothing to answer. When the sun goes down, he opens his heart before God, and earlier than that sun appears upon the hills he gives thanks for his protection during the night; for he feels that among men, become desperate by their danger, it is God only that can preserve him. He loves peace, and all that he had in store he has given to those who have been robbed by your people lest they should plunder the innocent to re-pay themselves. The whole season which others have employed in providing for their families, he has spent in his endeavors to preserve peace; at this moment his wife and children are lying on the ground, and in want of food; his heart is in pain for them, but he perceives that the Great God will try his firmness in doing what is right.

Father! The game which the Great Spirit sent into our country for us to eat is going from among us. We thought that he intended we should till the ground with the plough, as the white people do, and we talked to one another about it. But before we speak to you concerning this, we must know from you, whether you mean to leave us and our children any land to till. Speak plainly to us concerning this great business.

All the lands we have been speaking of belonged to the Six

Nations, and no part of it ever belonged to the King of England, and he could not give it to you.

The land we live on, our fathers received from God, and they transmitted it to us for our children, and we cannot part with it.

Father! We told you that we would open our hearts to you. Hear us once more.

At Fort Stanwix, we agreed to deliver up those of our people who should do you any wrong, that you might try them, and punish them according to your law. We delivered up two men accordingly, but instead of trying them according to your laws, the lowest of your people took them from your magistrate and put them immediately to death. It is just to punish murder with death; but the Senecas will not deliver up their people to men who disregard the treaties of their own nation.

Father! Innocent men of our nation are killed one after another, and our best families; but none of your people who have committed the murders have been punished.

We recollect that you did not promise to punish those who killed our people, and we now ask, was it intended that your people should kill the Senecas, and not only remain unpunished by you, but be protected by you against the revenge of the next of kin?

Father! These are to us very great things. We know that you are very strong, and we have heard that you are wise, and we wait to hear your answer to what we said, that we may know that you are just.

ADDRESS

OF

PRESIDENT WASHINGTON TO CORNPLANTER, DEC. 29, 1790.

The reply of the President of the United States, to the Speech of THE CORNPLANTER, HALF-TOWN *and* GREAT TREE, *Chiefs and Counsellors of the Seneka Nations of Indians.*

I, the President of the United States, by my own mouth, and by a written Speech, signed by own hand and sealed with the seal of the United States, speak to the Seneka nation, and desire their attention, and that they would keep this Speech in remembrance of the friendship of the United States.

I have received your Speech with satisfaction, as a proof of your confidence in the justice of the United States—and I have attentively examined the several objects which you have laid before me, whether delivered by your Chiefs at Tioga Point, in the last month, to Colonel PICKERING, or laid before me, in the present month, by THE CORNPLANTER, and the other Seneka Chiefs, now in Philadelphia.

In the first place, I observe to you, and I request it may sink deep in your minds, that it is my desire, and the desire of the United States, that all the miseries of the late war should be forgotten and buried forever. That in future the United States and the Six Nations should be truly brothers, promoting each other's prosperity by acts of mutual friendship and justice.

I am not uninformed that the Six Nations have been led into some difficulties with respect to the sale of their lands since the peace. But I must inform you that these evils arose before the present government of the United States was established, when the separate States and individuals under their authority, undertook to treat with the Indian tribes respecting the sale of their lands.

But the case is now entirely altered—the general government only has the power to treat with the Indian nations, and any treaty formed and held without its authority, will not be binding.

Here then is the security for the remainder of your lands.— No State, nor person, can purchase your lands, unless at some public treaty held under the authority of the United States. The general government will never consent to your being defrauded. But it will protect you in all your rights.

Hear well and let it be heard by every person in your nation, that the President of the United States declares, that the general government considers itself bound to protect you in all the lands secured you by the Treaty of Fort Stanwix, the twenty-second of October, one thousand seven hundred and eighty-four, excepting such parts as you may since have fairly sold to persons properly authorized to purchase of you.

You complain that JOHN LIVINGSTON and OLIVER PHELPS have obtained your lands, assisted by Mr. STREET, of Niagara, and they have not complied with their agreement.

It appears, upon inquiry of the Governor of New York, that JOHN LIVINGSTON is not legally authorized to treat with you, and that every thing he did with you has been declared null and void, so that you may rest easy on that account.

But it does not appear from any proofs yet in the possession of government, that OLIVER PHELPS has defrauded you.

If, however, you should have any just cause of complaint against him, and can make satisfactory proof hereof, the Federal Courts will be open to you for redress, as to all other persons.

But your great object seems to be the security of your remaining lands, and I have, therefore, upon this point, meant to be sufficiently strong and clear.

That in future you cannot be defrauded of your lands.—That you possess the right to sell, and the right of refusing to sell your lands.

That, therefore, the sale of your lands, in future, will depend entirely upon yourselves.

But that when you may find it for your interest to sell any parts of your lands, the United States must be present by their agent, and will be your security, that you shall not be defrauded in the bargain you may make.

It will, however, be important that before you make any farther sales of your land, that you should determine among yourselves who are the persons among you that shall give such conveyances thereof as shall be binding upon your nation, and forever preclude all disputes relative to the validity of the sale.

That, besides the before-mentioned security for your land, you will perceive by the law of Congress for regulating trade and intercourse with the Indian tribes—the fatherly care the United States intend to take of the Indians. For the particular meaning of this law I refer you to the explanations given thereof by Colonel PICKERING, at Tioga, which, with the law, are herewith delivered to you.

You have said in your Speech, "That the game is going away from among you, and that you thought it the design of the Great Spirit that you till the ground;—but before you speak upon this subject, you want to know whether the United States means to leave you any land to till?"

You now know that the lands secured to you by the Treaty of Fort Stanwix, excepting such parts as you may since have fairly sold, are yours, and that only your own acts can convey them away. Speak, therefore, your wishes on the subject of tilling the ground. The United States will be happy to afford you every assistance in the only business which will add to your numbers and happiness.

The murders which have been committed upon some of your people by the bad white men, I sincerely lament and reprobate, and I earnestly hope that the real murderers will be secured, and punished as they deserve. This business has been sufficiently explained to you here, by the Governor of Pennsylvania, and by Colonel PICKERING, on behalf of the United States, at Tioga.

The Senekas may be assured, that the rewards offered for apprehending the murderers will be continued until they are secured for trial, and that when they shall be apprehended, that they will be tried and punished as if they had killed white men.

Having answered the most material parts of your Speech, I shall inform you, that some bad Indians, and the outcast of several tribes who reside at the Miamee Village, have long continued their murders and depredations upon the frontiers lying along the Ohio. That they have not only refused to listen to my voice inviting them to peace, but that upon receiving it they renewed their incursions and murders with greater violence than ever. I have, therefore, been obliged to strike those bad people, in order to make them sensible of their madness. I sincerely hope they will hearken to reason, and not require to be further chastised. The United States desire to be the friends of the Indians, upon terms of justice and humanity.— But they will not suffer the depredations of the bad Indians to go unpunished.

My desire is that you would caution all the Senekas and Six Nations, to prevent their rash young men from joining the Miamee Indians.—For the United States cannot distinguish the tribes to which bad Indians belong, and every tribe must take care of their own people.

The merits of THE CORNPLANTER, and his friendship for the United States, are well known to me, and shall not be forgotten, and as a mark of the esteem of the United States, I have directed the Secretary of War to make him a present of two hundred and fifty dollars, either in money or goods, as THE CORNPLANTER shall like best—and he may depend upon the future continued kindness of the United States;—and I have also directed the Secretary of War to make suitable presents to the other Chiefs present in Philadelphia;—and also, that some further tokens of friendship to be forwarded to the other Chiefs, now in their nation.

Remember my words, Senekas—continue to be strong in

your friendship for the United States, as the only rational ground of your future happiness, and you may rely upon their kindness and protection.

An agent shall soon be appointed to reside in some place convenient to the Senekas and Six Nations. He will represent the United States. Apply to him on all occasions.

If any man brings you evil reports of the intentions of the United States, mark that man as your enemy, for he will mean to deceive you and lead you into trouble. The United States will be true and faithful to their engagements.

GIVEN under my Hand and the Seal of the United States, at Philadelphia, this twenty-ninth day of December, in the year of our Lord one thousand seven hundred and ninety, and in the fifteenth year of the Sovereignty and Independence of the United States.

GO. WASHINGTON.

BY THE PRESIDENT:
TH. JEFFERSON.

SPEECH OF CORNPLANTER,

IN REPLY TO PRESIDENT WASHINGTON'S ADDRESS.

FATHER:—Your speech, written on the great paper, is to us like the first light of the morning to a sick man, whose pulse beats too strongly in his temples and prevents him from sleep. He sees it and rejoices, but is not cured. You say that you have spoken plainly on the great point. That you will protect us in the lands secured to us at Fort Stanwix, and that we have the right to *sell*, or to *refuse* to sell it. This is very good. But our nation complain that you compelled us at that treaty to give up too much of our lands. We confess that our nation is bound by what was there done; and acknowledging your power, we have now appealed to yourselves against that treaty, as made while you were too angry at us, and therefore unreasonable and unjust. To this you have given us no answer.

Father! That treaty was not made with a single State—it was with the Thirteen States. We never would have given all that land to one State. We know it was before you had the great authority, and as you have more wisdom than the commissioners who forced us into that treaty, we expect that you have also more regard to justice, and will now, at our request, re-consider that treaty, and restore to us a part of that land.

Father! The land which lies between the line running south from Lake Erie to the boundary of Pennsylvania, as mentioned at the treaty at Fort Stanwix, and the eastern boundary of the land which you sold, and the Senecas confirmed to Pennsylvania, is the land in which HALF TOWN and all his people live, with other Chiefs who always have been and still are dissatisfied with the treaty at Fort Stanwix. They grew out of this land, and their fathers grew out of it, and they cannot be persuaded to part with it. We, therefore, entreat you to restore to us this little piece.

Father! Look at the land which we gave to you at that treaty, and then turn your eyes upon what we now ask you to restore to us, and you will see that what we ask you to return *is a very little piece*. By giving it back again you will satisfy the whole of our nation. The Chiefs who signed that treaty will be in safety, and peace between your children and our children will continue so long as your land shall join ours. Every man of our nation will then turn their eyes away from all the other lands which we then gave up to you, and forget that our fathers ever said that they belonged to them.

Father! We see that you ought to have the path at the carrying-place from Lake Erie to Niagara, as it was marked down at Fort Stanwix, and we are all willing that it should remain to be yours. And if you desire to reserve a passage through the Conewago, and through the Chatauque lake, and land for a path from that lake to Lake Erie, take it where you best like. Our nation will rejoice to see it an open path for you and your children while the land and water remain. But let us also pass along the same way and continue to take the fish of those waters in common with you.

Father! You say that you will appoint an agent to take care of us. Let him come and take care of our trade; but we desire he may not have any thing to do with our lands; for the agents which have come among us, and pretended to take care of us, have always deceived us whenever we sold lands; both when the King of England and the States have bargained with us. They have by this means occasioned many wars, and we are, therefore, unwilling to trust them again.

Father! When we return home we will call a Great Council, and consider well how lands may be hereafter sold by our nation. And when we have agreed upon it, we will send you notice of it. But we desire that you will not depend on your agent for information concerning land; for after the abuses which we have suffered by such men, we will not trust them with any thing which relates to land.

Father! There are men that go from town to town and beget children, and leave them to perish, or, except better men take care of them, to grow up without instruction. Our nation has looked round for a father, but they found none that would own them for children, until you now tell us that your courts are open to us as to your own people. The joy which we feel at this great news so mixes with the sorrows that are past, that we cannot express our gladness, nor conceal the remembrance of our afflictions. We will speak of them at another time.

Father! We are ashamed that we have listened to the lies of LIVINGSTON, or been influenced by the threats of war by PHELPS, and would hide that whole transaction from the world, and from ourselves, by quietly receiving what PHELPS promised to give us for the lands they cheated us of. But as PHELPS will not pay us even according to that fraudulent bargain, we will lay the whole proceedings before your court. When the evidence which we can produce is heard, we think it will appear that the whole bargain was founded on lies which he placed one upon another; that the goods that he charges to us as part payment were plundered from us; that if PHELPS was not directly concerned in the theft, he knew of it at the time and concealed it from us, and that the persons that we confided in were bribed by him to deceive us in the bargain, and if these facts appear, that your court will not say that such bargains are just, but will set the whole aside.

Father! We apprehend that our evidence might be called for as PHELPS was here, and knew what we have said concerning him; and as EBENEZER ALLEN knew something of the matter, we desired him to continue here. NICHOLSON, the interpreter, is very sick, and we request that ALLEN may remain a few days longer, as he speaks our language.

Father! The blood which was spilled near Pine creek is covered, and we shall never look where it lies. We know that Pennsylvania will satisfy us for that which we spoke of to them before we spoke to you. The chain of Friendship will now, we hope, be made strong as you desire it to be. We will hold it fast, and our end of it shall never rust in our hands.

Father! We told you what advice we gave the people you are now at war with, and we now tell you, that they have promised to come again to our towns next spring. We shall not wait for their coming, but will set out very early and show to them what you have done *for us*, which must convince them that you will do for them every thing which they ought to ask. We think they will hear and follow our advice.

Father! You give us leave to speak our minds concerning the tilling of the ground. We ask you to teach us to plough, and to grind corn; to assist us in building saw mills, and to supply us with broad axes, saws, augers, and other tools, so as that we make our houses more comfortable and more durable; that you will send smiths among us, and above all, that you will teach our children to read and write, and our women to spin and to weave. The manner of your doing these things for us we leave to you, who understand them; but we assure you we will follow your advice as far as we are able.

SPEECH
OF
CORNPLANTER, HALF TOWN, AND BIG TREE, SENECA CHIEFS.
ON TAKING LEAVE OF PRESIDENT WASHINGTON.

FATHER! No Seneca ever goes from the fire of his friend until he has said to him, "I am going." We, therefore, tell you, that we are now setting out for our own country.

Father! We thank you from our hearts, that we now know there is a country we may call our own, and on which we may lay down in peace. We see that there will be peace between your children and our children, and our hearts are very glad. We will persuade the Wyandotts, and other western nations, to open their eyes and look towards the bed which you have made for us, and to ask of you a bed for themselves and their children, that will not slide from under them. We thank you for your presents to us, and rely on your promise to instruct us in raising corn, as the white people do; the sooner you do this the better for us. And we thank you for the care you have taken to prevent bad men from coming to trade among us. If any come without your license we will turn them back; and we hope our nation will determine to spill all the rum which shall hereafter be brought to our towns.

Father! We are glad to hear that you determine to appoint an agent that will do us justice in taking care that bad men do not come to trade among us; but we earnestly entreat you that you will let us have an interpreter, in whom we can confide, to reside at Pittsburg. To that place our people, and other nations, will long continue to resort. There we must send what news we hear, when we go among the western nations, which we are determined shall be early in the spring. We know JOSEPH NICHOLSON, and he speaks our language so that we clearly understand what you say to us, and we rely on what he says. If we were able to pay him for his services we would do it, but when we meant to pay him, by giving him land, it has not been confirmed to him; and he will not serve us any longer, unless you will pay him. Let him stand between us we entreat you.

Father! You have not asked any security for peace on our part, but we have agreed to send you nine Seneca boys to be under your care for education. Tell us at what time you will receive them, and they shall be sent at the time you shall appoint. This will assure you that we are indeed at peace with you, and determined to continue so. If you can teach them to become wise and good men, we will take care that our nation shall be willing to receive instruction from them.

SPEECH OF CORNPLANTER,

TO PRESIDENT WASHINGTON, PHILADELPHIA, FEBRUARY 28, 1797.

FATHER! I thank the Great Spirit for protecting us through the various paths which we have trod since I was last at this place. As I am told you are about to retire from public business, I have come to pay my last address to you as the Great Chief of the Fifteen Fires, and am happy to find that I have arrived here in time to address you once more as father, and to advise with you on the business of our nation. You have always told us that the land which we live upon is our own and that we may make such use of it as we think most conducive to our own comfort, and the happiness of posterity.

Father! I wish, whilst I am able to do business, to provide for the rising generation. Our forefathers thought that their posterity would pursue their tracks, and support themselves by their hunts, as they did in the extensive forests given them by the Great Spirit, and by them transmitted to us. But the great revolution among the white people in this country has extended its influence to the people of my color. Turn our faces which way we will, we find the white people cultivating the ground which our forefathers hunted over, and the forests which furnished them with plenty, now afford but a scanty subsistence for us, and our young men are not safe in pursuing it. If a few years have made such a change, what will be the situation of our children when those calamities increase?

Father! To those points I wish to draw your attention, and once more to have your candid and friendly advice on what will be the best for the present race, and how we can best provide for posterity. Your people have a different mode of living from ours; they have trades and they have education, which enables them to take different pursuits, by which means they maintain themselves, provide for their children and help each other.

Father! I am also told that your people have a strong place for their money, where it is not only safe, but that it produces them each and every year an increase without lessening the stock. If we should dispose of part of our country and put our money with your's in that strong place, will it be safe? Will it yield to our children the same advantages after our heads are laid down as it will at present produce to us? Will it be out of the reach of our foolish young men, so that they cannot drink it up to the prejudice of our children?

Father! You know that some of our people are fond of strong drink, and I am sorry to observe that your people are too apt to lay that temptation before them.

Father! The last time I was here I mentioned to you that my mind was uneasy in regard to Mr. OLIVER PHELPS'S purchase, to which you desired me to make my mind easy, and said that you would inquire into the business. On my return I met Mr. PHELPS at Canandaigua, where he promised to give me a piece of land and to build me a house, and give me some cattle. With this I was satisfied, till I saw him again sometime after, when he, to my surprise, had almost forgotten it; but when I put him in mind of it, he gave me a horse and ten cattle, but refused the house and land because land had raised so much in value.

Father! To one thing more I wish your attention. When I was returning home the last time I was here, I was plundered by some of your unruly people of several things, amongst which was a paper, given me by General PARSONS, entitling me to one mile square of land at Muskingum, which I have never been able to recover, and without your friendly assistance must lose the land.*

---

* This is the land granted by the Ohio company referred to in Colonel SNOWDEN'S Historical Sketch. It thus appears that CORNPLANTER'S title papers for this land were stolen from him.

Father! I congratulate you on your intended repose from the fatigues and anxiety of mind which are constant attendants on high public stations, and hope that the same good spirit which has so long guided your steps as a father to a great nation, will still continue to protect you, and make your private reflections as pleasant to yourself as your public measures have been useful to your people.

SPEECH OF CORNPLANETR,

TO THE GOVERNOR OF PENNSYLVANIA, FEBRUARY, 1822.

I feel it my duty to send a speech to the Governor of Pennsylvania at this time, and inform him of the place where I was from, which was at Connewaugus, on the Genessee river. When I was a child I played with the butterfly, the grasshopper and the frogs; and as I grew up, I began to pay some attention, and play with the Indian boys in the neighborhood, and they took notice of my skin being of a different color from theirs, and spoke about it. I inquired of my mother the cause, and she told me that my father was a residenter in Albany. I still eat my victuals out of a bark dish. I grew up to be a young man, and married me a wife, and I had no kettle nor gun. I then knew where my father lived, and went to see him, and found he was a white man, and spoke the English language. He gave me victuals while I was at his house, but when I started home, he gave me no provision to eat on the way. He gave me neither kettle nor gun, neither did he tell me that the United States were about to rebel against the government of England.

I will tell you, brothers, who are in session of the Legislature of Pennsylvania, that the Great Spirit has made known to me, that I have been wicked; and the cause thereof has been the Revolutionary war in America. The cause of the Indians being led into sin at that time, was that many of them were in the practice of drinking and getting intoxicated. Great Britain requested us to join with them in the conflict against the Americans, and promised the Indians land and liquor. I myself was opposed to joining in the conflict, as I had nothing to do with the difficulty that existed between the two parties. I have now informed you how it happened that the Indians took a part in the Revolution, and will relate to you some circumstances that occurred after the close of the war.

General PUTNAM, who was then at Philadelphia, told me there was to be a Council at Fort Stanwix; and the Indians requested me to attend on behalf of the Six Nations, which I did, and there met with three commissioners who had been appointed to hold the Council. They told me that they would inform me of the cause of the Revolution, which I requested them to do minutely. They then said that it originated on account of the heavy taxes, that had been imposed upon them by the British government, which had been for fifty years increasing upon them; that the Americans had grown weary thereof, and refused to pay, which affronted the King. There had likewise a difficulty taken place about some tea, which they wished me not to use, as it had been one of the causes that many people had lost their lives. And the British government now being affronted, the war commenced, and the cannons began to roar in our country.

General PUTNAM then told me at the Council at Fort Stanwix, that by the late war, the Americans had gained two objects: they had established themselves an independent nation, and had obtained some land to live upon, *the division line of which from Great Britain run through the Lakes.* I then spoke, and said I wanted some land for the Indians to live on, and General PUTNAM said that it should be granted, and I should have land in the State of New York for the Indians. He then encouraged me to use my endeavors to pacify the Indians generally, and as he considered it an arduous task, wished to know what pay I would require. I replied, that I would use my endeavors to do as he requested with the Indians, and for pay therefor, *I would take land. I told him not to pay me money or dry-goods, but land.* And having attended thereto, I received the tract of land on which I now live, which was presented to me by Governor MIFFLIN. I told General PUTNAM that I wished the Indians to have the exclusive privilege of the deer and wild game, to which he assented. I also wished the Indians to have the privilege of hunting in the woods and making fires, which he likewise assented to.

The treaty that was made at the aforementioned Council, has been broken by some of the white people, which I now intend acquainting the Governor with. Some white people are not willing that the Indians should hunt any more, whilst others are satisfied therewith; and those white people who reside near our reservation, tell us that the woods are theirs, and they have obtained them from the government. The treaty has also been broken, by the white people using their endeavors to destroy all wolves, which was not spoken about in the Council at Fort Stanwix, by General PUTNAM, but has originated lately.

It has been broken again, which is of recent origin. White people get credit from Indians, and do not pay them honestly according to agreement. In another respect, also, it has been broken by white people residing near my dwelling; for when I plant melons and vines in my field, they take them as their own. It has been broken again, by white people using their endeavors to obtain our pine trees from us. We have very few pine trees on our land in the State of New York, and whites and Indians often get into dispute respecting them. There is also a great quantity of whiskey brought near our reservation, and the Indians obtain it and become drunken.

Another circumstance has taken place which is very trying to me, and I wish for the interference of the Governor. The white people who live at Warren, called upon me some time ago, to pay taxes for my land, which I objected to, as I never had been called upon for that purpose before; and having refused to pay, they became irritated, called upon me frequently, and at length brought four guns with them, and seized our cattle. I still refused to pay, and was not willing to let the cattle go. After a time of dispute, they returned home, and I understood the militia was ordered out to enforce the collection of the tax. I went to Warren, and to avert the impending difficulty, was obliged to give my note for the tax, the amount of which was forty-three dollars and seventy-nine cents. It is my desire that the Governor will exempt me from paying taxes for my land to white people; and also to cause that the money I am now obliged to pay, be refunded to me, as I am very poor. The Governor is the person who attends to the situation of the people, and I wish him to send a person to Allegheny, that I may inform him of the particulars of our situation, and he be authorized to instruct the white people in what manner to conduct themselves towards the Indians.

The government has told us, that when difficulties arose between the Indians and the white people, they would attend to having them removed. We are now in a trying situation, and I wish the Governor to send a person authorized to attend thereto the forepart of next summer, about the time that the grass has grown big enough for pasture.

The Governor formerly requested me to pay attention to the Indians, and take care of them. We are now arrived at a situation in which I believe the Indians cannot exist, unless the Governor should comply with my request, and send a person authorized to treat between us and the white people the approaching summer. I have now no more to speak.

www.ingramcontent.com/pod-product-compliance
Lightning Source LLC
Chambersburg PA
CBHW020139170426
43199CB00010B/812